There Is Something Wonderful
in the State of Denmark

There Is Something WONDERFUL in the State of DENMARK

by Arne Melchior

Translated by Esther Aagaard Tapelband

LYLE STUART INC.

SECAUCUS,   NEW JERSEY

Published by Lyle Stuart, Inc.
120 Enterprise Ave., Secaucus, N.J. 07094
In Canada: Musson Book Company
A division of General Publishing Co. Limited
Don Mills, Ontario

Queries regarding rights and permissions should be
addressed to: Lyle Stuart, 120 Enterprise Avenue,
Secaucus, N.J. 07094

Manufactured in the United States of America

ISBN 0-8184-0429-9

Preface

One of the most famous classical children's books in Denmark is called *The Escape to America*. It describes how a small boy, tired of his mother's more or less justified scoldings, decides to run away from home and head for the country of his dreams: America. However, he never gets further than to the curb, as his mother has forbidden him to cross the street!

Luckily, quite a few of us have visited each other's streets since then. We have worked, studied and vacationed with each other, and the air bridge across the Atlantic has been constantly expanding. Some Danes know a lot—and a lot know something—about the U.S. This is hardly surprising, as the U.S. plays a leading role in the world, is our major partner in NATO, and is one of our biggest trade partners. News about your domestic situation is abundant and, to make the picture complete, we watch American soap operas on Danish TV!

Of course the American public does not have a similar opportunity to learn what is going on in little Denmark. This is a shame, because what we lack in quantity, I believe we have in quality.

I do hope that this book will give you the impression that I just might be right in this assertion, and that your curiosity will make you feel like getting to know us better.

—Poul Schlüter
Prime Minister of Denmark

Contents

Contents

There Is Something Wonderful
in the State of Denmark

Introduction

When I meet Americans in the U.S. or at home in Denmark, they often ask me: "Are you related to Lauritz Melchior?" Then, when I have to say no, they tend to be a little disappointed. They would so much like to know someone related to "The great Dane." Americans over fifty still remember this Danish-born stately, heroic tenor from the Metropolitan Opera and movies.

However, I am "only" related to my own family, which came to Denmark in the sixteen hundreds. In various ways members of this family came to play a considerable part in Danish business life, in law, and as rabbis for the Jewish community in Copenhagen (rabbis who were known throughout the country and abroad).

The Danish people is an unusually homogeneous

one with a long continuous history on its own soil. Still, this nation has received a wealth of input from abroad—partly through immigration, partly from Danes who travelled abroad and found inspiration.

Also the Danes have been justly known for being level-headed people. To a certain degree this is still the case. We are not taken in by popular leaders or seducers of crowds. Healthy skepticism and critical sense endure. However, the changes brought about by the technological revolution after the Second World War have not passed without leaving some traces.

Tendencies to extreme points of view and to violence have also found their way to our country. However, stability and the ability to make compromises continue to be a predominant Danish characteristic.

Denmark is the link between Northern Europe (Scandinavia) and the European continent. Geographically Denmark has become a good springboard for Americans discovering Europe—a gateway to the continent. Here one can study some of the best qualities and relics of "the old world."

Profile
of the Danes

There has never been a revolution in Denmark, and it may be said with some certainty that none will ever occur. (Though, of course, we have some parties calling themselves revolutionary!)

The Danish climate simply makes a revolution impossible. Our location between the North Sea, the Cattegat, and the Baltic leaves us vulnerable to completely unexpected and strong showers at any time, and who can walk about in the streets demonstrating and making revolution while holding an opened umbrella?

Also, there are those who feel that the lack of revolutionary possibilities is due to the fact that the Dane

15

must have his hot dinner at the latest by six-thirty—and if you are not finished with the revolution by dinner time, you might as well let it go!

That business about the showery weather being an obstacle to revolution is more than a joke. It is a fact that the Dane's blood never really gets to boil. When he manages to work himself up and really starts to get wild and hot, in comes a fresh wind and a shower from the sea. Blood and temperament cool down quickly, and gone are all thoughts of overthrowing the government.

A nation is not just a product of its history and traditions. A people's manners and character are determined, first of all, by its climate and geography.

In Denmark summers are usually not unbearably hot, and winters are not bitingly cold. Like our temperature, so we are ourselves: not warmblooded, not cold—rather, lukewarm. Not too much and not too little—but a soft in-between. Not yes-yes! and not no-no!—but something like: Possibly. Let us look at it, let us talk about it. . . .

Looking at our geography, several things are apparent. As mentioned, we are surrounded by sea, sound and channel. Our only land frontier (with Germany) is a little more than 44 miles. Thus we mainly have to travel over water to visit others. Our closest neighbors are fish and herring, and you don't have much trouble with them. Said differently: We are islanders with all of their peculiar characteristics. We are homebodies, resourceful, and quite convinced that we know best.

When we look at the map, two other facts emerge: Denmark is small in area, and the land is flat.

Once we were much larger, indeed! A thousand

16

years ago the Vikings landed on the British Isles. Later a Danish queen gathered the Nordic countries under her crown (this was 600 years ago), and Danish kings have ruled Scandinavia for centuries. Danish troops have fought in Estonia and far down on the European continent.

Then we had a king, Christian IV, who ruled from 1588-1648 and involved Denmark in a goodly number of wars—each at the wrong time and on the wrong side! This was when the country started to grow smaller and smaller. Finally we were really small, and our poets learned to make a virtue of necessity. They praised our smallness as charm: "What is lost on the outside, must be won on the inside."

The last time we lost land was after a war with Germany in 1864. We got some of it back after the Versailles peace treaty. But we were still small, and small we remain. "Small is beautiful," as the Americans would say. We *are* small, and we enjoy it!

It should be mentioned that the said king Christian IV was very popular in spite of all the lost wars. For one thing, he was personally brave; for another, he built many beautiful castles and churches; and finally, he had a folksy nature, loving life and all its delights.

His contemporaries as well as future generations showed no resentment over the lost areas but considered him to be a true king of the people. You see, we Danes are not suited to be imperialists. We don't need grandeur and heroism. We prefer that which is cozy, cheerful, and charming.

That our area is small is also reflected in our horizons, which are somewhat narrow. The Dane can be narrow-minded. The lack of square miles and the non-existing masses of people make us somewhat provincial—in the less flattering sense of the word. We have enough in our own, and we are skeptical towards those who are different.

Also, as mentioned, Denmark is a flat country—no mountains, no rocks. One of the highest points in Denmark is 466 feet above the sea, and it is typical that we call this (very beautiful) place "Himmelbjerget"— The Sky Mountain. We Danes don't get much closer to the sky! The highest point in the country is 564 feet above the sea.

Just as the country is flat, so can the Dane be somewhat "flat." Without large, uninhabited expanses, eternal snow and wild mountain landscapes, or the opportunity for lonely walks on mountain peaks, there is an absence of mysticism, deep visions, and lofty inspirations.

Under these circumstances, we have few philosophers, although Søren Kirkegaard is justly world famous, and Harald Hoffding is well known.

Summa summarum: The Dane is lukewarm, narrow-minded, unenthusiastic and provincial!

This, of course, is far from the whole truth. Such a description is an excessively unfriendly interpretation. So why not give a friendly interpretation?

It won't be difficult. The physical circumstances just described have kept the Dane in balance—not too much, and not too little, but just right. He has found the golden mean in dealing with his fellow man. He is neither gushing nor reserved, but reasonable and tolerant.

He is neither high-flying (sanguine) nor speculative (melancholic), but straightforward and cheerful. "To stay on the earth—this serves us best" is a famous line of a Danish patriotic song.

Several positive, charming aspects are connected with Denmark's physical nature. The smallness of the country and people makes it wonderfully easy to take us all in. We understand each other, and because we are uncomplicated, it is easy for foreigners to understand us. The lack of masses of people gives importance and dignity to the individual. A *Herrenvolk* mentality cannot exist in Denmark.

The climate, too, has charm. One need not fear getting sunburned. We do not suffer a merciless sun and thus do not become lethargic or unable to work because of the heat. We can work during the noon hour. On the other hand, we can take off early in the afternoon and enjoy the long summer evenings and the light northern nights (June, July and August). In the winter, while there is little skiing, it also does not freeze much, and the nation does not spend much time or energy clearing snow.

For want of minerals and other natural resources, we have been forced to become skilled in the working and refining of imported raw materials. This is why Danish design, furniture, silver, jewelry and handicrafts have attained a leading position on the world market.

As manufacturers and designers, and with our considerable commercial fleet, we have also developed quite a business talent. If you need a good salesman, look for him in Denmark.

19

A friend from Sweden told me of a Dane and a Swede who became partners in a business venture. The basis was that the Swede had the money and the Dane the experience. After six months the partnership was dissolved—the situation had been reversed.

We compensate for our lack of natural riches with a certain matter-of-fact attitude; we are pragmatic and unceremonious among ourselves and in our relationship with our fellow man. This is not very original, but it is both practical and pleasant.

Altogether, great originality is not a Danish characteristic, though there is inventiveness and adaptability.

Denmark forms a link between the Scandinavian peninsula and the European continent. Many have passed through us to reach others, and we ourselves have tailed along on the travels. For centuries it was a tradition that Danish journeymen, after finishing their training, would go "waltzing"—i.e., they went travelling for some years to work abroad and gain experience, after which they would return enriched.

This was also the case for our artists and other intellectual workers. All our best thinkers, writers, painters, sculptors, et al.—in the past as well as in the present—have spent great parts of their lives outside our borders, especially in Southern Europe.

There the light of the sun was stronger, and there was more elbow room; things were larger and more international. There you found genii and eccentrics, and there the Danes met creative people from many countries.

The Danes absorbed and brought back impressions

and experiences. This was also the case with political currents and new thoughts. Not everything brought home could be used in the form it had been found. However, as mentioned, the Danes are practical people. We have the ability to translate foreign ideas and experiments into Danish and adapt them to Danish conditions. We soften and adjust the thoughts, knock off the sharp edges, and add a Danish mildness, smile and lack of pomposity.

One important example of such a transformation process in Danish history was the emancipation of the peasants. Until 1788, feudalism was the order in Denmark. The peasants were serfs of the landowners and the nobles. They had to remain where they were born, and most of the fruit of their labors had to be delivered to the owner of the estate.

But the Danes knew how to listen and how to catch the new signals from the great foreign lands. And the year before the French Revolution we had gone so far that our peasants were emancipated, serfdom and feudalism were abolished. Contributing to this was the fact that some German nobles in our government were instrumental in adapting the new thoughts to Danish use.

Again the Danes showed their evolutionary abilities. Soft, smooth transitions instead of bloody and violent revolutions—a rare example in the history of the world of the privileged giving rights to the suppressed without a revolution.

The blending of Danes and foreigners has taken place smoothly and without great problems. If you leaf through Danish history books or today's Danish telephone books, the multitude of foreign names tells of a great importation of human material. As it is for the people, so it is for the royal house.

Our queen's grandfather found his queen in Germany, and she became as Danish as anyone—for instance in her resistance to the Nazis. The queen's father found his queen in Sweden, and she is still adored by the entire nation. Our queen herself found her Prince Consort, Count Henri, from France. They all make our genealogical tree look good. We assimilate them, and they us.

The Danish stock takes well to grafts. We have a blend of people different from the American; we have understood how to utilize the best experiences from home or from abroad. And the new has adapted harmoniously to our thousand-year-old history and traditions.

Denmark and Its Monarchy

Denmark elected its first Social Democratic prime minister in 1924. After a break from 1926 to 1929, he formed a government again. His name was Thorvald Stauning; he was a professional cigarmaker.

On the program of the Social Democratic Party was—and still is—the abolition of the kingdom and the establishment of a republic. But this is only on paper. In reality the party has never even tried to make an effort to fulfill this point in its program.

This, of course, is because the Danes love their royalty.

The criticism heard most often from the limited

number of readers of the principal Social Democratic paper, *Aktuelt*, is that there are too many negative comments about the royal family. Lately, the editors have taken the consequences, and the paper now speaks very positively about the royal house.

In the beginning of the nineteen thirties, Prime Minister Stauning was asked why he did not try to carry through with the abolition of the kingdom. He gave two answers: First, he said, the king (at that time Christian X) would be elected president anyway if Denmark became a republic, so we might as well keep calling him king!

Secondly, said Stauning, we have the kingdom arranged so sensibly that if the king is clever, skillful and charming, he can do a lot for the country. But should he be not very clever, sick, or otherwise unfortunate, he can't do much harm!

Luckily, the Danish monarchs have been both clever and skillful for the last couple of centuries. Also the royal house have known enough to keep up with the times.

This is a difficult balancing act. The monarch must be majestic, and exalted and thus keep a certain distance. At the same time he or she must be accessible, charming and preferably popular. The Majesty must be a guarantor of traditions and at the same time validly reflect the nation's present and future. To the Danes, "the Royal house is history's red thread" (a quotation from an interview with our present queen, Margrethe II).

Margrethe's mother, Swedish-born Ingrid, is given a great deal of credit for the modernization of the royal

house. To an unusual degree she has understood how
to keep the difficult balance between high dignity and
sympathetic warmth.

From the thousand-year-old list of kings, let us
mention Frederik VII (he was king from 1848-1863).
He relinquished absolute monarchy and gave Denmark
its first free constitution in 1849. His motto was: "The
people's love is my strength."

After him came Christian IX. Difficult after-effects
of the absolute monarchy showed up during his reign.
Representative democracy made its way slowly. It was
not easy for him to adjust to the new time, but he did
manage to get the people's respect and love. He became
known as "Europe's father-in-law." One daughter became queen of England, another tsarina of Russia. A
grandson was elected king of Norway, another king of
Greece.

Christian X was king from 1912 to 1947, during
both World Wars. He had much authority, and during
the Second World War he emerged as the unifying
rallying point of the nation. Every morning Christian X
rode on his horse through Copenhagen, and tourists
from all over the world were practically dumbfounded
to see the king ride about, without any guard whatsoever, surrounded by bycyclists and other traffic, stop-
ping for red lights and greeting everyone. They called
him "Christian, beloved by the people."

His son, Frederik IX, ruled from 1947-1972. He
was "the Sailor King" with a thorough maritime training; all his life he showed the frank bluffness
characterizing the people of the sea. He was very mu-
sical, and on several occasions he directed the Royal Or-

chestra. Together with Queen Ingrid, he became the reformer who introduced the royal house to the modern era. His motto was: "With God for Denmark."

His daughter is Denmark's present ruling queen, Margrethe II. She inherited a firm religious attitude from her parents, and has many talents. She has been a practicing archeologist, she translates from French (with her husband, Prince Henrik, french-born Count Henri de Monpezat), and she has illustrated several books. One year the queen designed the postal Christmas seals, and in 1985 she designed a stamp marking the fortieth anniversary of Denmark's liberation from Nazi occupation.

Queen Margrethe has vast knowledge of history and culture. On this basis she has given many frank TV interviews at home as well as on visits abroad, and her yearly TV speech on New Year's Eve is in no way clichéfilled but attempts to give a genuine picture of the nation's spiritual state of affairs at the turn of the year. This has caused a great deal of dicussion, but much more admiration.

According to the constitution the monarch has no political liability, and his or her person is sacred. Consequently the royal house does not interfere in political matters. The monarch appoints the leader of the government, but entirely according to parliamentary rule. The prime minister keeps the queen informed about government matters, but the ministers do not discuss political questions with the queen, who is above the law.

The queen signs the laws adopted by parliament and only then are they in force.

On May 26, 1986, when the queen's eldest son,

Frederik, turned 18, he became the actual crown prince and took a seat in the "Statsraad" (consisting of the queen and the cabinet ministers). In time he will succeed Queen Margrethe as King of Denmark with the name of Frederik X. The red thread of history is assured continuation.

The Danish royal house has succeeded in maintaining its status as a symbol for the nation. Just as the flag is our national rallying point only by virtue of the people's need and acceptance, so is the queen and the royal family the personified rallying point, the neutral common denominator, which everyone acknowledges.

Denmark and Democracy

The Danish parliament (since 1953, unicameral) has a very special name. It is not "Reichstag" or National Assembly—nothing ceremonious or distinguished. It is just the "Folketing"—which means something like "the people's council." The Folketing is the place where the people's representatives negotiate society's affairs.

Thus we call our form of government "the People's Rule." It is a government by and for the people. It is not a government by the elite.

As for honesty, diligence, intelligence, knowledge, creativity, etc., the members of parliament as a whole are a suitable representation of the qualities found in the general population.

28

Accordingly the Danes do not pay its members of parliament or its cabinet ministers especially high salaries. As in other Scandinavian countries, England, and the Benelux countries, the idea is that those who administer the laws should not have a standard of living different from that of the population whose interests they are to safeguard—a healthy ideal.

It is typical that the Danish electoral system is the work of a Frenchman. The system is mathematically accurate. One can be quite assured that if a party gets, for instance, 15 percent of the votes, then it will also have 15 percent of the seats in the Folketing.

Another significant charm of our system is that no votes are wasted. In this it is neither like the English nor the American system. In the U.S.A., if a party's candidate gets more than 50 percent of the votes in a constituency, then the rest of the votes are wasted. Americans call this "majority rule." I call it "winner takes all."

The only condition for a Danish party's getting complete proportional representation is that it must have at least 2 per cent of the total votes.

In Denmark we find it important that a voter be assured that his vote is included in the total apportionment so that he does not risk falling into a minority whose votes are simply lost. In return, the Danish voters show up in large numbers. There is nearly a 90 per cent voter turnout for most Folketing elections. Eligibility and the right to vote commences in the eighteenth year.

In this system, votes that do not lead to election in a certain constituency are added up for distribution into the so-called supplementary seats. Out of the 175 seats of the Folketing (plus two from Greenland and two from the Faroe Islands), 120 are divided into the individual constituencies, while the remaining 55 are apportioned into supplementary seats. In this way mathematical accuracy is obtained.

The electoral period is four years, but at any time the prime minister can dissolve the Folketing and issue writs for a new election. This happens very often in the middle of an electoral period. Thus one could say the members of the Folketing are always on three weeks' notice. The cabinet ministers can be replaced at the prime minister's pleasure, and in principle their term of notice is a mere three hours!

Denmark has a lively diversity of parties. It must sound like a joke to the very populous democratic countries that eight to ten parties usually are represented in the Folketing. This, of course, gives a very diversified political picture, and it can be difficult to form a majority government.

During most of the years after the Second World War Denmark has thus been ruled by minority governments. Under this system a government can continue to govern as long as a plurality is not *against* it.

A minority government is not possible in many countries. Naturally such a government is not always as effective as a majority government. But the main requirement of democracy is not effectiveness either. The main requirement of democracy is consideration.

When a government is not based on a majority in parliament, things take longer to accomplish. One has to negotiate—consider the other sides—in order to get the needed plurality for a law. This can be a cumbersome process, but on reflection, this situation is really a democratic ideal. A minority government can never "shoot" or threaten its way through; it has to negotiate. And negotiation is a democratic ideal. Democracy is talk.

A Danish party is naturally much more homogeneous than one in, say, the U.S.A., Australia, England, France or Germany. In the large democracies the parties are often divided into wings or factions. Democratic voters in the Northern states of the U.S.A. often have different opinions from the same party's voters in the Southern states. In Denmark it is not like that.

The well-known "isms" are not enough to handle the tasks in a dynamic world, full of tension and renewals. Be it capitalism, liberalism, socialism or communism, all of these social programs are more than a hundred years old. Not one of them has the answers to the onrushing questions of our time. In our opinion it is not a great advantage for a political party to be able to boast of great age. Youth, renewal and experiments are needed to meet the challenges. Otherwise society easily becomes too static.

Just as we speak of—and practice—the People's Rule, so we talk of the People's School and the People's Church. The Danish educational system will be described in a special chapter of this book. There you will read of freedom and the influence of parents.

Thus Denmark does not have a State church, but a People's church. Paragraph 4 of the constitution says, in so many words: "The Evangelical Lutheran Church is the Danish People's church and thus supported by the state."

We have a church minister in our government who has certain administrative responsibilities in regard to parochial legislation on church councils and the use of churches, etc. But the church lives its own life, theologically ruled by the bishops and administratively and economically governed by the church councils chosen by the people.

The Danish People's church has liberty of ministry and a great deal of leeway. Most Danes are automatically (through baptism) members of the People's Church and pay a special church tax. However, only a minority go to church regularly. You might describe Denmark religiously as rather lukewarm. If you ask the Danes, however, if they believe in God, most will answer yes.

For the rest, complete freedom of religion prevails. Catholics, Jews and Muhammadans and many others are exempt from the church tax and freely exercise their religions; they are respected and admitted to all professions. Only the monarch must belong to the People's Church according to the constitution.

The Elected and the Electors

It is easy to understand why citizens of authoritarian governments (which most governments are) are very critical towards those who rule their state. The rulers have seized power and forced themselves upon the people. They suppress freedom, use power, and do not allow the people complete fulfillment. Also, they cannot be removed without violence.

It is definitely less logical—yes, outright crazy—that citizens of the free nations, the democracies, are very critical towards their politicians. In a democracy it is the citizens (the voters) themselves who have chosen the politicians and given them the mandate, and, in the same way, these citizens can vote out the politicians on the next election day.

The political trade does not enjoy a very good reputation. "It became politicized," people say, and this means something like, "The matter became messy— something went wrong, it was not handled objectively."

I will describe in short what happens in Denmark; I think this description corresponds to what happens in other democratic countries. In this respect the Danes are not special.

There is excitement and atmosphere when we have an election; on election day itself there is almost joy; in some places they even raise the flag (they don't do this often enough in Denmark).

There is good reason to celebrate the occasion, for we belong to the privileged nations where free citizens elect their representatives and delegates by secret votes. No censorship, no force, no thought control—indeed something to be happy about.

The day after the election we still have a good atmosphere. The elected are congratulated, the losers receive condolences. The papers carry leading articles of the great expectations we have of the newly elected popular assembly.

This positive atmosphere lasts for about three weeks. Then the chase starts anew, led by certain papers. Dejection sets in again.

You see, the voters had succeeded in finding 179 of the laziest scoundrels and the most incompetent and corrupt persons to be found in the entire country! At least this is what the media tell us. Well, we must forgive the people. It is human to err. Only it is so amazing that it happens every time. This is almost unforgivable.

What is the matter with those voters? Are they really so dumb and uncritical that each time they are seduced into voting for the wrong people?

Not at all, not only are the people sovereign, they are also highly informed, and—at least in the case of Denmark—in possession of a healthy skepticism and critical sense. You cannot fool the voters every single time. Their judgment is correct and cannot be appealed.

In Denmark we have a perfect national register, which means that every single citizen receives a poll card enabling him to exercise his voting right. And in Denmark we have have one of the highest voter participation records of the free world. Between 85 and 90 per cent of all the citizens vote. (Only in Russia do they reach higher—there they are almost above 100 per cent).

If the voters do not like the system or the candidates, then they can stay at home. Here we call such people "Sofa voters," but we don't have very many of them. People show up every time, and they don't even make the silent protest by returning blank ballots.

This record-high participation in elections must be a clear proof that the voters accept the system and its players. The voter knows that by marking his ballot he exercises his sovereignty, and he naturally votes for parties and people with whom he identifies.

Thus the composition of parliament is the right one, of course; the one on which the voters have decided, consisting of the right people with the right attitudes and opinions. When I say "right," I refer to the fact that the viewpoints of the elected correspond exactly to the electorate's points of view.

In a democratic society one cannot continue to throw mud at one's politicians, or the criticism would become a boomerang. If the elected are wrong, then the voters must be so as well. Otherwise they would have elected somebody else!

Our country's wise fathers and mothers are not in the parliament. If they were we would have government by the elite, and we do not wish that. We want, and we have, government by the people. The people and the politicians must look at things about the same way—this is what is meant by democracy and rule by the people.

Nor is there any reason to be skeptical towards the politician's trade. Politics can be best translated as "Society's housekeeping." Politics deals with attitudes, just as in the case of problems at home or in business. Society's accounts cover bigger numbers, but in reality the problems are identical.

At home we deal with where we live, how we arrange our home, how well or expensively we eat, how we educate our children, and how we guide them; with whom we want to associate, and from whom we want to stay away. Which books we want to read, where we want to go on vacation and how much we want to spend there, and how much we want to spend on presents. How we prioritize our time and our efforts.

Politics is all of this, and therefore politics is the same as society's housekeeping.

Politicians are accused of being "professionals." In Denmark we have another expression, "limpets" (clinging to their offices). These words are usually used in a derogatory way.

It seems to me acceptable that a politician makes a living from his work. Is there anything shady or wrong in that? Doesn't a leader or administrator of a business or organization receive a full salary if it is his full-time job? How else should he make a living?

In fact, a politician *should* be a "limpet." He hasn't become a candidate for the fun of it, or as a hobby! He is serious about it. He has a point of view, opinions and goals. He makes his abilities and his advice available to society. Through his candidacy he has lured the voters into using their voice through him; so, when he is elected, it must be his duty to represent his voters, and to fight for their ideals or opinions. This he can do effectively only by staying where he can have influence.

Also, the politician must be able to stand criticism, to keep his health—including his nervous system—in good order, so that he won't be knocked down from his "chair," away from influence; for that would mean failing his constituents.

In my opinion, the mudslinging at politicians is very much a media phenomenon. At any rate, after more than 12 years of political work, I find the reactions of the citizens to be exceedingly positive. Politicians get lots of letters, telephone calls and all kinds of personal inquiries. They have a very large area of contact. About 98 per cent of those who contact me do so in a pleasant, friendly and respectful manner—even those who are critical. From conversations with my political collegues of various parties I know that they experience the same thing in their contact with our citizens.

My message to journalists of all media is therefore that it is all right to be skeptical and critical, and also aggressive—better too much than too little, or we will have situations that exist in dictatorships. But do not sling mud. Attack the case, not the person.

And my message to political collegues with other views is: Let us discuss the issues—straight from the shoulder. Democracy is dialogue. Let us quarrel if necessary, let our opinions clash, and let us make our differences clear to the public. But let us respect each other's motives, and let us show tolerance of those who think differently from us. Things or people are not black and white—not simple, but complicated.

Beliefs, viewpoints, ideas may be philosophically intolerant (in conflict), excluding one another. But the bearers of the ideas—the men and women—need not therefore be intolerant of bearers of other, possibly contrary ideas.

King Christian X and the Star of David

In many parts of the world it is believed that Denmark's king, Christian X, during the Nazi occupation of Denmark, wore the yellow Star of David. This was the sign the Nazis required all Jews in Germany and the occupied countries to wear in plain view.

The story became known all over the world through Leon Uris's novel *Exodus*. In it a Danish girl, Karen, tells us that the king was the first to voluntarily have the Star of David sewn on all his clothes—in solidarity with the Jews.

The story is good, but it is not true. It cannot possibly be true because the Germans in Denmark never required the Jews here to wear the Star of David.

Leon Uris surely believed the story, which probably came about because King Christian was supposed to have told somebody at court: "If the Germans require Danish Jews to wear the Star of David, I want to be the first to do so."

But next to mathematical truth is poetic truth, and that is the one Leon Uris believed.

On this basis the story of King Christian and the Star of David can be considered authentic. In a dramatized, poetic form it gives a picture of the attitude of the king and the Danish people towards the numerically small part of the population which is Jewish. The number of Jews in Denmark is about 6,000, nearly all living in Copenhagen.

My father, who was chief rabbi Dr. Marcus Melchior, wrote in his memoirs that the Danish people's loving relationship with its Jewish group may not have been best expressed in their rescue of them by transporting them to Sweden in October 1943. For this world historic effort, which in itself was heroic, might have been the result of various motives in some of the participants: resistance to Nazism (an excellent motive), need for adventure, economic gain, or other. No, the best proof of the solidarity the Danes had with their Jews, came—wrote my father—with their return in 1945.

At that time the royal house, the government and parliament, the city council and other authorities, as well as the general population, neighbors, acquaintances, yes, even competitors, displayed such hearty rejoicing that no one could doubt the mutual genuine warm feelings and the unity of the nation.

There is still another proof of the noble feelings shown by the Danes in that dramatic situation. When the Jews fled, spontaneously and without planning, they left their residences with their contents and their businesses and companies with their assets.

Immediately private people as well as municipal authorities took steps to collect the abandoned property. Everything was put away safely.

Companies remained in business, safeguarding the interests of the absentees, and it hardly ever happened that anyone made free with the assets which had been left so suddenly. Upon the return of the Jews, everything was turned over to them in complete order.

The city of Copenhagen took care of the holiest treasures, the many Torah scrolls that were left behind. During the remaining part of the war, they were kept in the cellar of a church in inner Copenhagen, and never fell into the hands of the Nazis. Great was the enthusiasm when the Torah scrolls were carried back to their proper place.

Unlike other nations where Jews have resided Denmark has never had a real problem with anti-Semitism. The first Jews did not come to Denmark as refugees, but as invited guests. In 1622, King Christian IV sent a letter to the Jewish congregation in Amsterdam inviting some Jewish families to come and live in Gluckstadt, a town he had built as a business center to compete with Hamburg (Gluckstadt is now German).

Since then there have always been Jews in Denmark. The Jewish congregation in Copenhagen is esti-

mated to have started in 1684, and thus it celebrated its
300th anniversary in 1984, with the lively participation
of the queen and the royal house. The Jewish Day
School was established in Copenhagen in 1805; about
one-half of all Jewish children attend this school. The
large synagogue was inaugurated in 1833.

Thus, in April of 1933, it had its 100th anniversary.
In the fall of 1932, the king, Christian X, had promised
to be present at the anniversary. However, Adolf Hitler
had come to power in Germany on January 30, 1933.
According to the anecdote, some advisers from the foreign ministry tried to dissuade the king from going to
the synagogue on this day of celebration. King Christian
is said to have answered: "I will show the world how a
king behaves"—and he went.

Jews in Denmark—as in a number of other countries—have played a relatively important part in Danish
cultural life, in the Danish press, and in business and
banking. This also is true for the academic community.
In the 1980s, and for the second time in this century,
the University of Copenhagen has a Jewish president.

The editor-in-chief of Copenhagen's biggest daily
newspaper is Herbert Pundik. He is the grandchild of a
Jewish family who immigrated here from Eastern
Europe. Together with his wife and two sons he emi-
grated to Israel in the 1960s. (One of his sons fell in the
war of 1973.)

In 1969, the newspaper *Politiken* offered Herbert
Pundik the job as the paper's chief editor. He and his
family declined, as they did not want to give up Israel as
their home. *Politiken* then proposed he remain in Israel
and still be editor in Copenhagen. An agreement was

made whereby he would stay 20 days a month in Copenhagen, and the newspaper would pay all expenses thus
incurred. In this way he and his family could keep their
home in Tel Aviv. By now this unique arrangement has
been working for 19 years. Naturally, it says something
about Pundit's ability that he has been able to keep the
position under such circumstances. But it also says
something about *Politiken* and about Denmark that the
arrangement was begun and continued. I doubt that
anything like it could have happened in any other country.

Jews have not been very active in Danish political
life. Until 1982, there were only two Jewish cabinet ministers, both ministers of finance. The first one was
Edvard Brandes (a brother of the author and critic
George Brandes, who was famous in Europe). He was
minister before and during the First World War. In the
1960s, Henry Grunbaum was finance minister. However, neither one of these two wished to be directly
identified as Jews.

In September of 1982, the present Danish government was formed. It consists of 21 ministers, two of
whom are Jews. In both cases most people know that
they are Jews and that they identify themselves that
way. In my own case, it is quite evident, as I am the
grandchild of a former Danish chief rabbi, the son of
one, and my younger brother, Bent, has been the chief
rabbi since 1970. I have held numerous posts in Jewish
organizations, among them president of the Danish Zi-
onist Federation from 1975 to 1979, even while I was a
member of parliament.

My Jewish collegue is a professor, Dr. Isi Foighel.

Since 1982, he has been the tax minister. Earlier he was president of the Jewish congregation in Copenhagen, and in this connection he was among the leaders of Dansk Flygtningehjelp (Danish Refuge Assistance), whose president he was for a great many years.

It is typical of Danish mentality that prime minister Poul Schlüter did not hesitate in appointing two Jews to become ministers. It should be noted that this was in the fall of 1982, after the summer when Israel's campaign into Lebanon had given rise to some dormant anti-Semitic currents in many countries. Such tendencies did not find any appreciable echo in Denmark.

If someone asks me if there is anti-Semitism in Denmark, I answer definitely, "No." However, if someone asks me if there are any anti-Semites in Denmark, then I'll answer, "Yes, there are some." But they are so few and insignificant that they don't enter the picture—not even a tiny part of the picture.

It is not an opinion, but a concrete fact that Nazism at no time could find roots in Denmark. This in spite of the fact that Germany is our nearest neighbor and the only one to whom we are connected by land, and in spite of the fact that Denmark was occupied by the Nazis for five years.

Even in brave and democratic Holland there was a strong Nazi movement for a number of years. Our Norwegian sister nation fought bravely against the Nazis, but still suffered the fate of having a Norwegian, Vidkun Quisling, give a name to all traitors, the Quislings. He had worked closely with Fridtjof Nansen in the 1920s and had been minister of defense in the Norwegian government from 1931-1933. He was therefore

44

trusted, and used his career as a basis for taking over the post as prime minister during the Nazi occupation.

The Nazis never succeeded in gaining a foothold in Denmark. Their leaders had no influence whatsoever. Not one single person known in politics, unions, art, or organizational life was won over to Nazism. True, there was one special exception, the poet Valdemar Rordam, but at that time he was definitely senile.

Even the Germans acknowledged this state of affairs. They never tried to place a Danish Nazi in the government. They knew this would be perfectly futile. Many have tried to figure out why it was natural and inevitable that the Danes stayed totally free of Nazism and anti-Semitism (de facto also of Communism). To my eyes it is connected with the description of Danish mentality and psyche that I gave in the introductory chapter of this book.

The Dane is (relatively) tolerant. If I were to generalize, I would say the Dane is earthbound, balanced, self-ironic and considerably skeptical of ideologies and idealogues. The Dane finds shouters like Mussolini and Hitler ridiculous. It is difficult to seduce a Dane.

The Dane knows that he and his country are indebted more than most to foreign inspiration and influence. So even though our inborn skepticism periodically may make us behave reproachfully towards foreign groups, we quickly return to understanding and tolerance.

A society is almost always indebted to those who are different, to those who bring it special traditions and abilities. It is not an advantage for a nation to have a situation where everyone has the same opinion, eats the same dishes, sings the same songs, or believes in the same ideals. Of course there has to be a common denominator or preferably several—this is how the nation is formed—but it is usually those who deviate and the originals who advance society.

They know this in the U.S.A., the nation of immigrants. Through 1000 years of common history the Danes are much more homogeneous, and our smallness might make us somewhat petty and provincial as described by Hans Christian Andersen in his fairytale "The ugly Duckling." However, we are not world beaters. We are evolutionary and, as farmers, it is our principle to doubt revolutionaries.

The Danish Model

Is there a special Danish system, or "model"? I think so.

It is related, of course, to the so-called Scandinavian model, the one that many countries in postwar Europe have tried to imitate and approximate. Many in the U.S.A. also find it an example worthy of imitation.

The most important characteristic of the Scandinavian model is extensive social solidarity. We do not believe in abandoning the weak. Society tries to help even those citizens who are considered responsible for their own unfortunate situation. This will be seen in the special chapter describing our social system. The motto of this model of solidarity is that old, ill, and other weak citizens be picked up by the system so that few will feel outside it.

Class divisions fell away early in Denmark. Naturally we have our rich and our poor, our lucky and our unlucky. But our school system, tax system, and other arrangements prevent the really great differences.

This development came first of all to Denmark. In his memoirs from the beginning of the thirties, a former Finnish ambassador to Denmark told the following story:

One Saturday evening he went to a restaurant in Copenhagen with a guest. In those days it was a rule that on Saturday evening dinner jackets and long dresses were required in order to enter.

While he and his wife were dining, he saw prince Axel and his wife, princess Margaretha, enter the restaurant. The maître d' escorted them to their seats and they passed by the ambassador's table. Following etiquette, the ambassador and his wife got up, bowing and curtsying to the princely couple.

A little later another couple entered. They too were dressed festively. The ambassador thought he knew the man, who also was escorted to his table by the maître d'. As the new guests approached the ambassador's table he saw that it was his own chauffeur with his wife. He was amazed, and when the chauffeur couple passed the ambassador's table, he and his wife got up, bowing and curtsying to the chauffeur exactly as they had just done to the prince and princess.

This is how it was in Denmark 50 years ago. The

chauffeur came to the same restaurant where the prince and the ambassador went to have a good time on a Saturday evening. According to the Finnish ambassador something similar could not have happened at that time in Finland, Norway or Sweden.

As there is equality between the classes, so there is equality between the sexes. When I was a boy in the 1930s, only 20 per cent of married women worked outside the home. Now, and for a long time, more than 80 per cent of the women have full-time jobs outside the home.

Women have been franchised and eligible to vote in Denmark since 1915. This did not cause them to occupy 50 per cent of the seats in parliament, government or numerous other institutions as they seemed to be destined to. But for a long time equal pay for equal work has been the rule, and women do not usually feel discriminated against.

There is also a splendidly relaxed relationship between the sexes which has not spoiled the natural play between man and woman.

For a while, the world over, Denmark was thought of as a country where the relationship between men and women was very free. There was talk of loose morals, about half- or completely-naked women on the beaches, about pornography, etc. The increasing liberality in many countries, including a freer treatment of eroticism and sex life in books, plays, and films, has probably put a damper on the concept of Denmark as Sodom. We ourselves never considered it as such.

However, it is probably true that in these areas the

Danes have fewer taboos. "Relaxed" is the word that covers it. There is no doubt that, without creating a stir, one can permit oneself more "liberties" in Denmark than one can just a bit farther south in Europe.

The sensation surrounding this situation is a thing of the past. Sex education in our schools is obligatory, and between the sexes, as well as between the generations, there is a natural uncomplicated atmosphere which does not need to become flat or vulgar.

It has been a long time since women threw away the corset, and the bra is not fashionable among the young. Body consciousness without prurience is great in both sexes. It is just free and lovely.

The Danish lifestyle includes "hygge" and fun. "Hygge" is a Danish word which is almost impossible to translate. The dictionary says that it means "comfortable, snug, cozy, homelike, pleasant or nice." Not one of these words covers the whole concept; rather, it is a melding of them all. I am surprised that the dictionary does not mention "relaxed," for this adjective is included in the concept of "hygge" or "hyggelig." One can have "hygge" at home, while out with friends, in a restaurant or on a beach.

Speaking of beaches: Denmark has a coast line of 4,350 miles. This is quite a bit when compared to our total area of 16,633 square miles. Bathing on the free beaches is one of our great vacation joys and has probably brought about our free manners at the beach.

But back to our lifestyle and fun. One of the names given to Copenhagen is "The Paris of the North." Here many foreigners seem to find a certain elegance (not a heavy one, as in Germany or Sweden) and a light, fun-filled atmosphere.

Personally I think the Swedes are great fun. But I am rather alone in this opinion. The Swedes themselves, and also the Danes, find them much more stiff and formal. Everyone I meet says that lightness, perhaps a certain degree of unconcern (recklessness?), is typically Danish.

At any rate, we are not melancholic, but it is difficult to incite Danes to a high degree of enthusiasm. They would rather hear a joke than rally round a speaker; one can't keep a Danish audience awake very long, unless one spices up the presentation—even of serious subjects—with a witticism or a light remark.

I myself like this attitude, which is a natural one. There is an old saying that one need not be boring because one is serious.

There can be a lot of self-irony in Danish humor. Here is just one example:

A Frenchman, an Englishman and a Dane are in a bar discussing women. The Frenchman says: "The most gorgeous women are French. They have such splendid, long legs. Do you know how long their legs are? They are so long that when a French woman is sitting on a barstool she can reach the floor with her feet. And this is not because we have especially low barstools—they just have such long legs."

The Englishman says: "The most gorgeous women are English. They are so splendidly slender. Do you know how slender they are? They are so slender that if we put our arms around their waists, we need only our two hands to reach around. And this is not because we have especially long fingers—they just have such slender waists."

And the Dane says: "The most gorgeous women are Danish. They have such splendid behinds. Do you know how splendid their behinds are? If I leave home to go to work in the morning and give my wife a friendly smack on her behind, then her behind will still be shaking when I come home from work. And don't think it is because Danish women's behinds are so big. It is just that we have such lovely short workdays."

Our business world is also part of the "Danish model." This is better described in the chapter, "The Dane as Supplier." The Dane is a good salesman, partly because he has to be, partly because he is "fun" to deal with, and finally because he is generally very well-informed. This makes the visit of a Danish salesman a welcome one.

Danish design comes through in the entire process, from planning through production to sale and delivery.

A special feature of the "Danish model" is a system of joint venture between the private and the public sector. Denmark has a so-called mixed economy—i.e., it is not a pure form of Capitalism and not a pure form of Socialism, but, like the climate, something in between. This makes it possible to blend the large public sector's know-how and prestige with the private sector's boldness and creativity.

State-owned institutions combine with private companies to form a number of corporations. With such combined forces we have made the Danish business presence felt in a number of countries all over the world.

Denmark is probably the only country in the world where any citizen, without previous notice, has the right to call for a personal meeting with a cabinet minister. Every Thursday from 10 a.m. to 11 a.m., the cabinet ministers have open house (office hours). If a cabinet minister is away, or unable to be present, he must so inform the public at least two days beforehand.

Danish Habits— Good and Bad

Earlier I described the Danes as a bit cool, but don't think that they are unfriendly or unkind. As a Dane I do not see it as anything special, but almost every tourist I meet here extols the helpfulness and courtesy of the Danes.

It is obvious that it is easy to approach the Danes, and you never ask in vain for directions or little favors along the way. In certain areas their courtesy has no limits. This applies to invitations, for instance. When you are invited to a party, you naturally thank your host for the invitation. When you arrive, you say, "Thank you for asking me to come." After the meal, you say (to the host as well as to the hostess), "Thank you for the food," after the coffee, you say, "Thank you for the coffee," and when you leave the host family, you say, "Thank you for a lovely evening." The day after the party you call or write (according to the type and extent of the party), "Thank you for yesterday," and the next three or four times when you meet, you say, "Thank you for last time."

The hosts, for their part, repeat about as many times, "Thank you for coming!"

This is not all. When you leave the party, you also say, "Thank you for this evening" to the other guests, and during the following weeks you say, "Thank you for your company when we were together last," to those of the other guests you might run into.

Does this sound excessive? It is, but it heightens the pleasure of the party.

One arrives exactly on time to parties, meetings and gatherings. For dinner you may be as much as five minutes late, but not much more.

It is a German/Nordic rule that one arrives on the dot. This is a sign of good planning, and naturally it saves a lot of time and aggravation for everyone involved. The hostess can be sure that the roast is not over-done and that the soufflé does not collapse.

In parliament all meetings start on the dot, whether they be plenary sessions or committee, or other meetings. This sounds like strict discipline, but in fact it is just a question of organization.

The first time you visit a Danish home, flowers are a must. A box of chocolates may be substituted. If there are small children in the family a little chocolate or some small toy may do.

A small gift at arrival is usually given among families who see each other more often, but this can be varied in kind and size. A meal is usually started by the host rising to bid everyone welcome and introducing foreign guests or people who are in the home for the first time, and then comes the inevitable "Velbekomme" and "Skål." At the dessert, the guest who is seated next to the hostess rises to praise her and make a little "thanks for the food" speech. Of course this speech is also concluded with a "Skål."

Speeches for the ladies are quite rare, nowadays. This kind of speech went out of fashion in the name of equal rights. It might still take place at a New Year's Eve party, or at occasions where there is a little extra festiveness.

In a few homes where old virtues are appreciated, the meal also starts and ends with the mother's or father's "Velbekomme" (May the meal do you good). In our home we rarely skip it; also, it is not acceptable for anyone in the family to get up from the table without saying, "Thanks for the food," usually accompanied by a kiss for Dad as well as for Mom.

I don't think I trespass against this rule five times a year, and I recommend it as worthy of imitation. Perhaps there are those who say that when such things are done repeatedly they become superficial formalities. This may be true, but politeness costs nothing, and I find it as necessary as the salt on the potatoes. Also you don't enter a place without saying, "Hello," nor do you leave without saying goodbye.

"Skåling"—which takes place several times during a meal—is somewhat of a ceremony. It is not done just by raising one's glass and then drinking. You hold the glass towards the one with whom you want to "skåle," then the two of you look (with varying degrees of intensity according to whom you are "skåling" with) straight into each other's eyes. Then you drink. Then you hold the glass towards the person you are "skåling with," and the eye pantomime is repeated. Only then do you both put down your glasses.

Tipping was done away with in Denmark a long time ago. On the menus in hotels and restaurants it is stated that taxes and tips are included in the prices given. You should have this in mind when you compare them with prices in other countries.

In fact, waiters or waitresses do not expect tips. Nor do hair dressers, gas station attendants, taxi drivers or hotel receptionists. I will not claim that extra amounts are refused, but they are not expected, and they are generally considered to be out of fashion.

The philosophy is that service people are fairly paid nowadays, which makes tips appear patronizing and therefore offensive to those who are offered them. As mentioned before, class differences have fallen away, and we are more equal if we accept that the people who serve us are—like ourselves—doing their jobs and being paid accordingly. Of course, you need not take this too literally. Hotel porters or bellhops, among others, are still very interested in tipping. We aren't fanatics!

To most Danes biking is an everyday event. In Denmark (for 5.1 million inhabitants) we have one and a half million cars and about four million bicycles.

Denmark is ideally suited for bicycling. The country is flat, and in the towns there are no hills either. It is true the wind may be a little troublesome if it is against you, but it has its advantages in that the girls' skirts blow upwards, brightening the traffic picture in a delightful way.

The English say that one should never talk about money, at least they said so in "the good old days." Nowadays, I believe, even wealthy Englishmen cannot keep themselves from discussing money.

In Denmark, taxes are not just something one has to pay, they are something one discusses very much. And there is good reason for such a lot of the talk. Denmark is very high in global tax statistics. When one adds the direct and the indirect taxes, one wonders that the Danes have anything left for living expenses. In the nineteen thirties, we had a Minister of Finance (Vilhelm Buhl) who coined the slogan: "Pay your taxes happily." It would be an exaggeration to say that most Danes do so. You hear a lot of moaning, and it is true that just in my lifetime the tax rate has risen so many times that you would think we reached more than 100 per cent long ago.

This is not the case, however. In spite of high taxes and duties, the Danish standard of living is one of the highest in the world. And if you speak intimately with the Danes, most of them admit that they really get something for their tax money. The social safety net is closely meshed, and most people are very content with the peace of mind that is granted in daily life.

I don't think it is an exaggeration to say that countries with high taxes generally have the happiest inhabitants. At least they are safe, well organized and socially cohesive.

Many grumble if their buying power does not rise in one or more years. But, again, if you press the Dane, he will admit that he and his family have a relatively first-class living standard, whether compared to earlier generations or to conditions in other countries today.

In the meantime, you might think that the Danes are all optimists. We use and consume more and more—more than we can afford, that is, more than we earn. A few years ago a Norwegian politician said: "Economically the Danes are going to hell—but they are travelling there first class."

The record for Danish taxes is set by those on cosmetics, beer and alcohol, and on cars. The taxes on these products are called luxury taxes.

This is really a bad custom, and it is also a bad description. What is a luxury? Usually it is something my neighbor has and I do not have, either because I do not like it, or because I cannot afford it. Is lipstick a luxury? Or a "snaps"? Or a car? No, it isn't, is it?

In Denmark a car costs three times more than it is worth. If it is a very expensive car, the buyer is punished even more.

Tourists do not suffer much under these sad circumstances. They do not buy cars here, and as for the tax rate on the other goods, it may be a certain consolation that, since 1984, the Copenhagen International Airport has been the second cheapest in Europe for purchase of "luxury goods." The Copenhagen airport is embellished with the title "Gateway to Europe."

And then you can walk on one of the many wide, white beaches and look at naked people! The swimsuits gradually became so small that they weren't there anymore.

A few years ago one of my friends was visited by a young student as part of the youth exchange program of Rotary-regi. This young man came from Egypt. He was picked up in the airport and taken to the Danish family's summer house in North Sealand. After lunch everyone went down to the beach.

After a little while, the family heard shouting nearby. The young Egyptian had started to make advances to a young girl who was sunning herself—completely naked! The student, of course, had never seen anything like it—although maybe he had dreamt about it. He had undergone complete culture shock. It was with great difficulty that the Danish family got him away from the girl. His explanation was that to him the girl's natural state seemed like an invitation.

In reality the Danes are rather modest. They do not like to talk about faith or religion. *The Christian Daily*, an excellent newspaper, does not have a lot of subscribers, and if someone is reading it in the train, it is often folded so that the other passengers do not see that you are "one of those."

In regard to singing, the average Dane is also very discreet. Unfortunately the good old tradition of starting and concluding, for instance, political meetings with a song has died out.

While religion and singing have been "privatized," body awareness has grown so much that now even the less shapely appear on the beaches or at parties with the least possible amount of textile covering them.

The Nordic type is tall, well proportioned and blond. Yet you meet many "tubby" Danes. At least one-third of the Danes are overweight. This is because of their great joy of food—and, of course, because of their prosperity. Also, the beer adds to the intake of calories! In contrast to our Scandinavian brother countries, Denmark has no restrictions whatsoever in regard to the buying and serving of beer and alcohol. The only hindrance might be the high taxes, but lots of Danes submit voluntarily to this "punishment."

In regard to food, Denmark is one of the leading gastronomic countries. Not only do Danes eat a lot, but, usually, the food is very well prepared. Neither Norway, Sweden, Germany or England can measure up to Denmark. We have been famous for our "Smorrebrod" (open-faced sandwiches) for generations; justly famous also is the "Big, Cold Table," with four or five kinds of herring, salads, lots of meat spreads, warm dishes, and large varieties of cheeses, desserts and fruits; and it can still be had in beautiful dining places at very reasonable prices.

The hot dinners are also of a high quality. They may not be particularly Danish, but in many places all over the country you may have Italian as well as French dishes as excellent as those served in Italy or France. Also, here the Danish gift for importing good customs and even improving on them makes itself evident.

Dishes grouped under "Everything Good from the Sea" deserve a special mention. We have a number of special fish restaurants. According to my genuine gourmet friends, you may have here the best bouillabaisse in Europe as well as delightfully prepared fish, shell fish and all other gifts from the sea.

Fish are good for you and fish are cheap. And whatever we or our guests cannot eat, we can export. Our biggest customers are France, Italy and Spain. Every single day long rows of refrigerated trucks roll down across the continent with freshly caught fish.

Smoked fish is rightfully very popular. Smoked (or gravad) salmon, smoked eel, and—not to forget—the smoked herring from Bornholm belong to the finest delicacies of the Danish table.

In all countries food is part of the culture. If we are to be judged according to our eating habits, Denmark has a very highly developed culture. Meals are also part of the social culture. Measured this way, the high social standard is also confirmed.

Thus, things are interwoven. With a good meal you must have good drinks. With the herring and the cheese you need, first of all, a good aquavit. During the Second World War, "Rød Aalborg," "Jubilœum," and many other famous brands of Danish snapps became known as the Danes' secret weapon. Quite a few of the German Wehrmacht soldiers who were here occupying our country got too many snappses and went under the table—knocked out—and the German military police had to come and pick them up.

Danish snapps is strong as a Viking, fresh as a virgin, fiery as a suitor and cold as an iceberg.

We get our wine from Southern Europe. This we can't make ourselves. But the beer—the beer, friends! For good reasons it is world famous and can be bought almost all over the globe. The great Danish breweries can show enormous surplus profits. And everything that cannot be reinvested goes for—try to guess: Yes, the surplus goes to culture and to research! Large museums, costly art treasures, valuable exhibits, ballet tours, and numerous cultural activities and research programs are paid fully or in part by Carlsberg and Tuborg.

Think of this, too, the next time you get thirsty.

High schools in Denmark are not only educational teaching institutions where you may receive various types of advanced education. We also have a special concept called Folk High Schools.

A stay of three, six or ten months at a Folk High School is part of the Danish way of life. There, large numbers of the Danish population have received an essential part of their general education.

The idea of the Folk High Schools was introduced

in the 1830s by the minister, author and poet N.F.S. Grundtvig. Probably it is not wrong to consider the Folk High Schools the most important (some say the only) original Danish cultural product. It is also the largest Danish cultural export.

Since the Second World War, the Folk High Schools have gained a foothold in Germany, England and the U.S.A., and also in some African states and in India.

The dictionary defines the Folk High School as follows: A type of schooling (for adults) whose main aim is to provide the individual with background to enable him to understand and form opinions on society's problems and on universal human problems.

Classes are held in a free form on Danish and foreign languages, history, domestic and foreign literature, religion, psychology, economy, art, films, hobbies, gymnastics and many other subjects. There are professional, specialized high schools, agricultural high schools, athletic high schools, religious highs schools, etc.

The Folk High School is a legitimate child of the folk church. Just like the church, it receives support from the state without being the state school. It develops the citizens' individuality, which may be the most important quality of Danish life.

Copenhagen City Hall was built in the very first years of this century.

The Little Mermaid sits on her stone looking out at the harbor of Copenhagen. She is as famous as the Statue of Liberty in New York, but much smaller--and prettier. The tourists love her.

Christiansborg Castle in Copenhagen houses the Royal Reception Rooms, the Danish Parliament, and the Supreme Court.

Denmark's reigning queen, Margrethe II, has several artistic talents. In 1985 she designed a stamp to mark the 40th anniversary of the liberation from the Nazis. Here the author, as Minister of Transportation, Communication and Public Works, presents to Her Majesty the first copy of the stamp. On the left is Hans Wurtzen, General Manager of P&T.

Denmark has a coast line of 4,350 miles. White beaches are to found in many places. This is a beach on the sunshine island of Bornholm, the most easterly of Denmark's islands. Similar beach areas are to be found along the west coast of Jutland and North Zealand.

Strøget is the main shopping street in Copenhagen and the longest pedestrian street in Europe.

Kronberg Castle in Elsinore (28 miles north of Copenhagen) is one of the most interesting Renaissance buildings in Denmark. Shakespeare made it known throughout the world as the setting of *Hamlet*.

Centuries-old farm traditions still thrive alongside mechanization and modern design. Thatched and half-timbered farmhouses are still in good repair, some having been owned by the same families for generations.

Tivoli, the famous amusement park in Copenhagen, was opened in 1843. It is situated in the very heart of the city (that is City Hall in the background).

Legoland in Billund, Central Jutalnd, is a mini-world built of 30 million Lego toy bricks.

When the queen is in the capital, there is a changing of the Royal
Guards every day at 12 o'clock in the Amalienborg palace square.

The Old Town, Arhus,
is an open-air museum
founded in 1914 in part
of the Botanical Garden.

Every 4th of July a great Danish-American festival is held at the beautiful Rebild Hills (near Aalborg in northern Jutland) in which the Royal Family and a large audience participate. Many leading politicians and artists from the USA have spoken here.

Hans Christian Andersen's House in Odense, Funen, is a museum including collections of books, letters, papercuts, drawings and personal relics from the life of the famous writer.

Denmark has many bridges that are artistic masterpieces as well as engineering marvels. This bridge is part of the "bee-line" from Copenhagen to the Baltic. It was opened in 1985.

Denmark holds the leading position in the world in respect to wind energy. Ebeltoft in Jutland has the first sea-placed windmill park in the world.

The Dane as Supplier

No minerals or other riches can be found in the soil of little Denmark. We have found a bit of oil and a little natural gas in the part of the North Sea that belongs to Denmark according to International law. But these finds are trifles when you compare them to those of neighboring Norway and England.

So we have no riches to bore or dig for. Nor do we have large forests or water power. In return we have a fertile soil which rarely is in need of moisture. Here grain, grass, and non-exotic fruits and berries grow with great success.

Thus we have always been able to feed ourselves

with vegetables and also with meat, and we can sell more than we ourselves use.

Without natural resources, the Danes have been forced to work diligently, first as farmers and later in industry. Productivity is high, and so is general education and knowledge.

And then—you can trust the Danes. Not because we are better or more moral than others, but because we have learned that we are forced to be so. Instead of natural riches we have diligence and honesty.

In addition, we have developed a matter-of-fact business talent. The concept of "marketing" caught on early in Denmark.

The diligence of the Dane led to a high standard of living which we love very much. It means that we must have high wages, since everyone must live well and share in the high standard of living. This, again, made economic planning very important. The Danish workers' productivity is in the forefront of this planning.

Rarely are we cheapest, however. We compensate for this by well-thought-out quality and design. Factory-made products often maintain a standard that is craftsmanlike with designs of individual note. The beer, the furniture, the Lego bricks, the thermostats, the TVs, the dairy products, the canned fish, all combine distinguished traditions with sly inventiveness. Even the pig has become an "art" industry, when one considers the excellence of our pork products.

The Dane is first of all honest and precise—because he has to be! In practice this means that a contract is kept with scrupulosity. Time of delivery, quality, quantity and price from a Danish supplier is just about always as agreed upon. No deviation is tolerated. The Dane himself is critical of his suppliers, and this has taught Danish manufacturers to be very particular with their products and deliveries.

Prices without surprises! That is the Danish supplier's motto.

Visitors, and tourists to Denmark have the same experience with Danish merchants. Prices and agreements are kept, there are few complaints or disappointments. We cannot afford it.

In the last few years Denmark has again become one of Europe's least expensive capitals, and Copenhagen is among the most reasonable capitals in the world in regard to hotel—and food—prices.

For travelers from the U.S.A. to Europe or the Middle East, Copenhagen is right on the way. For those who can't resist the temptation to stay a couple of days in Copenhagen or in Denmark, it is very convenient that the Copenhagen airport has been rebuilt luxuriously, and has a large selection of goods which can compete price-wise with the cheapest duty-free prices in Europe.

In many Danish cities there are a great number of walking streets with many shops and a happy outdoor life with eating places, artistic decoration and a genuine "get together atmosphere."

Tivoli
(and Legoland)

This book is not a tourist book as such. It does not have chapters about the long lovely white beaches. We have barely mentioned that the west coast of Jutland is no less than a world sensation for vactioners, or that Copenhagen is "The City with the Many Beautiful Towers," or that in Odense you find the house where the story-teller Hans Christian Andersen was born (it has been made into a museum).

I have not mentioned the queen's picturesque guard or told of the many beautiful old manor houses, the impressive castle ruins, or the fully intact castles of the 16th century, or the Viking ships dug up from under the water, or about the 800 churches from the early Middle Ages with their invaluable frescos.

However, no book titled such as this is can be presented to the reader without mentioning Tivoli.

Every visitor to Copenhagen has heard about Tivoli, and anyone visiting between May 1 and September 15 has surely visited this park. What is so special and inspirational about Tivoli?

Several things must be mentioned.

First of all, Copenhagen is definitely the only capital of over a million inhabitants with an amusement park like this located right in the center of town. This big park is placed between Copenhagen's City Hall and the Central Station, simply on the most expensive real estate in the city. Still, it is open for only four and a half months. Secondly, Tivoli is unique in the number of amusements gathered at one place—from the most expensive to the cheapest (many entirely free), from the very noisy to the very quiet, from classic types to the most modern.

In Tivoli you find all the same attractions as in most other amusement parks around the world: merry-go-rounds, roller-coasters, roulettes, sail boats, shooting galleries, and many more.

Side by side and in between these hundreds of amusements—some even a little violent—is an outdoor pantomime theatre and a ballet which every single night give graceful plays and dances. There is a stage for circus performers, where fashion and sports shows are also held.

Around the park are a number of concert bandstands, and there is also a concert hall in modern classic

69

style. Every night a distinguished symphony orchestra performs here, and Tivoli's famed director, Niels Jorgen Kaiser, brings distinguished soloists and ensembles from all over the world to his concert hall.

All around are a great number of quiet areas where one can walk or sit on benches in the arms of one's sweetheart among beautiful flower arrangements and fountains.

Tivoli has more than 40 cafes and restaurants. Here you can have the most expensive and elegant food in the city, but you can also bring you own meal and sit at the tables and just buy drinks or coffee. Everyone can afford a trip to Tivoli.

An important attraction is the Tivoli Guard, a copy of the Royal Guard for boys only. It marches in a parade through the park and its orchestra performs on the outdoor stage.

Finally, I want to give one more explanation why Tivoli is so impressive. It is because everything—all buildings, amusements, indoor or outdoor arrangements—are kept in perfect order, newly painted and polished every single year. The entire area radiates quality.

Once I brought about a dozen foreign guests to Tivoli where we started with lunch. The plan was to stay in Tivoli for three to four hours. But they insisted on staying in the park till it closed at 12 midnight. They wanted to see "Tivoli by night" when the numerous lanterns and lighting arrangements evoke the most romantic atmosphere—as mentioned, in the very center of the big city.

Tivoli (and Legoland)

My guests were Englishmen and Americans of the most discriminating kind. They were widely travelled and quite wealthy. At the end of the evening, after having watched the grand display of fireworks, several of them commented something to this effect: "Though we have seen much beauty and magnificence around the world, don't think we can't be impressed. What we have seen today is one of the most beautiful and impressive things we have ever witnessed."

Many mayors from all over the world, and tourist agents from many countries, have stated they would go home and create a similar park in their homeland. No one has succeeded.

Tivoli was founded in 1849; it has traditions, a patina, and a distinction that cannot be copied. Tivoli is definitely the greatest attraction in Copenhagen in the summer, just as is the Royal Ballet in the winter season.

Now Jutland also has a unique amusement park. This is Legoland, founded, of course, by the family behind the world success, Lego bricks.

From the entire European continent tourists stream to Legoland, which can be compared to Disneyland and "Madurodam" in Holland.

From millions of Lego bricks entire cities have been built, true copies of famous buildings and monuments from all over the world, harbors, air ports, castles, etc. For the children there are many original activities which, in a pleasant way, entertain and teach at the same time.

In Legoland, too, it is easy to spend an entire day. One simply can't tear oneself away; and every year—

71

summer after summer—families from all over the country make Legoland a fixed part of their vacation program.

In Tivoli as well as in Legoland the high standard and the fine quality, carried through to the smallest detail, create an inspirational atmosphere which infects all visitors.

Here you find no drunks. Here you enjoy yourself fully with no other stimulant than elegance and good taste. Here you see how "Family Denmark" behaves when it is at its best.

Denmark in the World

The geographic role of Denmark as a connecting link between northernmost Europe and the European continent is also reflected culturally, socially and politically.

Denmark is the only country that is a member both of the Nordic Council and of the Common Market. For a long period of time, Denmark, in this double role, has carried out much appreciated work as intermediary between the north and south of Europe. Danish politicians and officials are messengers in both directions, which is a definite contribution to the harmonious workings among the nations of Europe.

In Denmark there is great popular sympathy for affiliation with the Nordic countries. The rivalry that existed for hundreds of years, especially between Denmark and Sweden, has long since been replaced by confidence and co-operation. Now it is mostly on the soccer field that we clash with each other.

The Nordic Council consists of Denmark, Sweden, Norway, Finland and Iceland. Participating are three autonomous territories (with home rule): the Aland Islands are included in Finland's delegation, and Greenland and the Faroe Islands are in Denmark's.

These five countries have been in the forefront of Europe in regard to hamonizing rules and regulations. Immediately after the Second World War, passport requirements were abolished, and since then a great number of laws covering marriage and divorce, social and tax matters, etc., have been adopted. Free movement of people, business and capital has been facilitated.

Before Denmark and Norway joined NATO, an attempt was made to establish a Nordic defense union. This did not prove feasible, and many were disappointed.

In reality, it is logical that Nordic countries could not get together on these matters in spite of the many historic and cultural connections. Finland borders with the Soviet Union, and thus its military freedom of movement is greatly limited. Sweden feels strongly attached to Finland, and, in addition, Sweden is almost as much in love with the politics of neutrality as is Switzerland.

This is why neither Finland nor Sweden wanted to join NATO, while the war experiences of Denmark and

Norway definitely called for a link with the great democracies of the Western World.

In 1972 referendums were taken in Norway and Denmark in regard to membership in the Common Market. In Norway a small majority was against this, but Denmark had a solid majority for the Common Market, and on January 1, 1973, Denmark, together with England and Ireland, became a member.

It is interesting to note that the Danish opponents of the Common Market were to be found in the groups that normally and principally advocated international co-operation. This pattern can also be seen in a number of other countries. Parties who stand up at meetings singing the Socialist battle song "The International" are precisely those who in practical politics end up becoming super nationalist, yes, even pure isolationists!

They make slogans and sing about international co-operation, but when it comes right down to it, they pettily and narcissistically try to keep to themselves.

In 1986 it thus became necessary to take a new referendum in regard to Denmark and the Common Market in connection with certain extensions of the Rome Treaty. The Common Market adherents won again, and since then all resistance to Denmark's membership in the Common Market has ceased. A similar situation can be found in England.

In contrast to the Nordic Council, a great number of decisions of the European Common Market are completely binding for its member countries. Therefore Denmark's membership in the Common Market is of much greater importance, in regard to its international orientation, than its membership in the Nordic family.

Most Danes hope very much that more of the Nordic countries eventually will join the Common Market. This may not be for a long time in the cases of Sweden, Finland and Iceland, but in Norway the debate has started again, and it would not surprise me if Norway applies for membership in the Common Market in about three to five years.

As already mentioned, Denmark is also a member of NATO. Here, too, we see the political left partly skeptical and partly directly antagonistic towards this alliance. However, all opinion polls show the population's steady majority for NATO. Also parliament shows the same majority—about 150 out of parliament's 179 members are supporters.

The large labor party—The Social Democrats—is also pro NATO, but the left wing of this party is flirting with the opponents. They speak a lot about Nordic zones free from nuclear weapons, and they try to limit appropriations to Danish defense.

Unfortunately this shows a petty, provincial attitude. They want the advantages of co-operation in the alliance, but would like to skip the obligations and get away as cheaply as possible in the membership. Indeed, this is not an especially noble attitude.

It is important that Denmark realizes its responsibility, and luckily the skeptics have not yet succeeded in hampering Denmarks reliability in the alliance.

In addition to membership in the Nordic Council, the Common Market and NATO, Denmark is, of course, also a member of the UN, of which they were co-founders in 1945.

There is a certain romanticism prevailing as to the

results the UN can obtain. It is therefore necessary to point out that the UN is unable to secure peace and progress in the overall picture. But, idealistically, a large common organization of (nearly) all the countries of the world is a positive matter, and if we did not have such an organization, we would have to hurry up and establish one.

Realistically, it is also very important that a forum exists where representatives of all nations may get together, bring out their differences, and learn from one another. For decades a great number of sub-organizations of the UN have had a particularly useful purpose in the development of various areas of the world.

To this end Denmark is constantly contributing fully in payments, co-operation and co-responsibility to the UN. For many years, Denmark has made troops available for the UN's peacekeeping forces in Cyprus. No one in Denmark would dream of shirking this kind of international obligation. Here it can also be mentioned that, through all these years, Denmark has been in the forefront in contributing to the Third World. We are among the five leading nations in the world when our financial contribution is measured in relationship to our Gross National Product.

At the same time it would be both unwise and naïve to attribute to the UN any direct possibility of preventing wars. No war (and there are many of them) has been avoided or terminated through the intervention of the UN.

Twice I have been a member of the Danish delegation at the UN's general meeting—in 1977 and in 1980. In 1980 the war between Iran and Iraq broke out, and the UN secretary general expended great effort to stop the war at the beginning by getting the foreign ministers of the two countries to meet at the Security Council.

He was successful in getting the meeting arranged, and I was present at the meeting in the Security Council, where the spokesmen for the two countries were literally sitting back to back. The powerlessness of the UN was shown by the fact that the meeting did not result in any kind of progress, and since then the UN has not played any visible part in efforts to end the war.

The UN must be considered an important international forum where everyone can meet, and where contacts can be made or cultivated. We must have such a place—as long as we have no illusions about its powers.

A war breaks out or continues only as long as one nation finds it to its advantage. To prevent or end wars or disputes between nations depends entirely on the parties involved, and, in addition, on the possible influence of the great powers on the said states. This kind of thing takes place—now as before—on a bilateral basis.

National vs. Global

In the fall of 1962, Prime Minister David Ben-Gurion made an official visit to Copenhagen. He desired that one Sunday morning be reserved for a meeting with young Jews from the Nordic countries. The arrangement was in the hands of the Scandinavian Jewish Youth Alliance, whose president I was.

About 150 Jewish youth leaders from Finland, Norway, Sweden and Denmark had gathered, and as president I had the treat of sitting with Ben-Gurion on the platform for 3-½ hours. The prime minister appeared to be a good listener, and his responses were complete and clear.

A young girl from Stockholm asked: "What are you first—a Jew or an Israeli?

Ben-Gurion replied: "I do not like this question, which I have heard before. It really isn't a reasonable one, for one might just as well ask a person if he is a child of his father first or of his mother. A reasonable answer can hardly ever be given to this question.

"But," continued Ben-Gurion, "I want to answer anyway. If I have to prioritize, then I am first and foremost a Jew, and next an Israeli."

He gave the following reason: To be a Jew is a moral and ethical affiliation—to be an Israeli is "only" a question of national affiliation. Were clashes to arise between these two affiliations, the moral/ethical affiliation would take preference over the national. These were strong words from the leader of a young nation.

Rounds of applause followed this answer, and I, too, found it to be a very fine one. Before calling upon the next person, I said: "Thank you for your answer, Mr. Prime Minister. I hope you will be happy to hear that this is the same reply I give to the question, when I attend meetings around the country."

Ben-Gurion interrupted: "If I were a Christian Dane, and you answered me like that, I would tell you that then you do not belong in Denmark, but in Israel." I answered him: "Then Israel's Prime Minister differs from the tolerant Danish people. For my countrymen find my answer to be all right, and it does not make them doubt my Danish patriotism."

The above exchange illustrates the old problem of

"double loyalty." How many completely loyal alle-
giances and affiliations can the individual handle?

It is my opinion that, in this area, the individual
also has enormous opportunities and possibilities. We
all know that our loyalties cover large areas. One can
love one's father and mother, one's sisters and brothers
and one's grandparents as well as one's friends and a
great number of relatives. To these are added, later,
one's mate, children and grandchildren. In fact, it is
easy to care deeply for a lot of people; the love for one
does not detract from the love for the others.

Man's ability to love, care for, respect and be loyal is
almost infinite. It can be compared to a living candle.
The flame of one candle can light an enormous number
of other candles without losing its ability to give light or
heat.

It is only when there is conflict between one's areas
of loyalty that the problems arise. In case of a divorce,
loyalty conflicts arise for the child. If two of one's
friends quarrel, one may have to make a difficult choice
as to which to side with.

In fact, Ben-Gurion's (and my own) answer to the
question of priorities and loyalties when divergencies
arise between the national and the ethical (global), has a
counterpart in recent Danish history.

In the fall of 1943, when the Nazis tried to arrest
and deport the Danish Jews, protests came in from
many places, from official authorities, from large organizations, etc. Among the protesters was also the Danish Church.

When the plans became known, the Danish bishops
gathered and sent out a pastoral letter that was mailed

81

to all Danish ministers and read loud during the services the following Sunday, October 3, 1943. The bishops' declaration concluded with the following words:

"The leaders of the Danish Church clearly understand their duty to be law-abiding citizens who do not offer misplaced opposition to those in authority. But we are also conscience bound to uphold justice and protest any violation of rights. We therefore must acknowledge that we must obey God before man."

When these words were read, the congregation in many churches arose spontaneously with an "Amen."

"Obey God before man!" These were strong words considering the situation, courageous words, for the bishops and the ministers clearly risked reprisals from the Germans.

"Obey God before man!" These are words of the clergy, which in layman's language has the same meaning as Ben-Gurion's answer: The ethical/moral comes first, if (unhappily) the matter should be put to the test.

Denmark and America

Denmark is a small, homogeneous country; a small territory with only five million people who are closely connected by virtue of a long common history and tradition.

The U.S.A. is a large non-homogeneous country; a territory spanning an entire continent, a very large and mixed population, a young and new nation when measured with the long gauge of history.

Denmark's strength is in her harmony, the strength of the U.S.A. lies (somewhat dramatically expressed) in her disharmony. This should be considered to be a positive statement. Of course, I am thinking of the variety of origin, culture, and traditions brought to America from all over the world.

Greeks, Italians, Germans and British are large elements of the population of the U.S.A., together with Norwegians, Swedes and Danes. The great example of the U.S. to the world—at least this is how we see it—is the nation's wonderful ability to adapt and integrate groups of people of highly different origins. The U.S.A. is the great melting pot where discrepancies are ironed out, and where individuality is allowed to survive under a common national umbrella.

This great variety has given the U.S. her resilience and strength, which has formed a great deal of the background for U.S.A.'s leadership in technical, scientific and cultural developments.

Most Danes look up to the U.S. I daresay we admire the ability this country has to bridge differences without obliterating the characteristics of the individual person or group.

Conformity in thought and behavior will always lead to mental poverty. This we see in all dictatorships. But small nations, in their provincial outlook, also run the risk of excessive homogeneity at the expense of individuality.

This is why the example of the U.S.A. is so important and precious to us.

Like the rest of Europe, Denmark owes a debt of gratitude to the U.S.A. For one thing, the U.S.A. has received, hospitably, many of our former citizens as well as immigrants from other countries. Without the openness of the U.S.A. through generations, the countries of

Europe would have had considerable pressure from homeless refugees.

But what counts most of all is the U.S.A.'s example as a freedom-loving nation. It is the opportunity available to the individual, family, group, or business there which is an essential example to all the nations.

To this can be added the U.S.A.'s contribution to the freedom of the European countries. In the First as well as the Second World War, the Allied nations received crucial moral, economic and military support from the U.S.A. One does not want to imagine what Europe would be today if the U.S.A. had stood back from the fray, dignified and isolationist.

Of course, we are not going to be naïve in this area either. Naturally the U.S.A. did not back us up for the sake of our blue eyes. We are not *that* blue-eyed. The U.S.A. also derived advantages from her efforts in the wars and in the alliances. But to me and to most Danes there is no doubt that the U.S.A. in a genuine brotherly way, and based on her great love for freedom and democracy, sacrificed her sons and her strength in an altruistic way as well.

That self-interest went hand-in-hand with this general interest did not make the effort less valuable.

The U.S.A. has had the bitter lesson that ingratitude is the way of the world, and that military help, the Marshall Plan, and war-preventing efforts often have damaged, rather than helped, its reputation in the rest of the world. This is how unjust things often are on the world stage. Of course, nations are no better than their people.

Also in Denmark—I should say *even* in Denmark—
there have been certain periods when such tendencies
came to the fore under the slogan "Ami go home." But
fortunately I can state that these were held by only a minority of our people and only for short periods.

The dominating feeling for the U.S.A. is one of
deep respect and sincere gratitude. There are many
proofs of this.

Every year, Denmark celebrates the 4th of July at a
large open-air meeting at the Rebild Hills near Rold
Forrest by Aalborg in North Jutland. The first was held
in 1912; thus these open-air meetings celebrated their
75th anniversary in 1987. Each year the royal family
participate with thousands of others, and the meetings
are broadcast over Danish TV.

Many important Americans have been speakers at
these meetings; at random we can mention: Ronald
Reagan, Maureen Reagan (1986), George Bush, Richard M. Nixon, Hubert Humphrey, Richard Netter,
Walter Cronkite, Art Buchwald, Walt Disney, Danny
Kaye, Victor Borge and Donald Petersen (Ford Corpo-
ration).

Denmark is the only country where such a tradition
and declaration of solidarity with the U.S.A. can be
found.

To us it is a happy fact that Denmark is a member
of NATO. When I sleep well at night, it is to a large degree because I feel safe knowing that my family, myself,
and all my countrymen enjoy the protection of the
U.S.A. through this alliance. Imagine if the U.S.A.
backed out and left Europe to her own devices! That
would be the end of my peaceful sleep at night.

Just imagine if the U.S.A. pulled back her forces from Europe. The European countries would then be forced to call in many more of their youth for military service, and military costs would rise like comets. Too many forget this in daily life.

Or all of Europe would be "Finlandized." Finished would be our freedom of being master of our own house.

Everyone understood this in the years after 1945. We all remembered that without the U.S.A., Nazism and Fascism would have won in Europe. Now we are faced with the authoritative power of Communism, and the threat of subjection under a system whose declared purpose is world domination and suppression of personal freedom.

But now there are those who think that one dictatorship is better than the other. Did they forget what European disarmament and neutrality in the thirties led to! History lessons have been remiss. The old people have forgotten, and the young ones have not learned enough. Romanticism is spreading.

War has never been averted by absence and weakness. This is shown in our thousand-year history. War can be averted only through presence and strength.

They can call this a cold war view, but if the cold war can keep away the hot one, then it is absolutely useful.

Many of the romanticists also try to criticize the idea of "balance of terror." It is true that it sounds bad when the word "terror" is part of an idea. Therefore the so-called "friends of peace," who want to remove the balance of terror, irresponsibly advocate that the

West—the free world—should start by setting a good example.

If this were allowed, the result would be that *the balance* is done away with, while *the terror* remains. Then we would have an unbalanced terror, and it does not take a great deal of imagination to imagine what would then happen. . . .

The SAS Airline Model

All nations attach great importance to their airline systems because of the prestige involved. Each European country has its own national airline company. Though its airlines are declining in numbers, the U.S.A. has a profusion of companies, which must be seen in light of the fact that the U.S.A. spans an entire continent. In comparison with Europe, however, the U.S.A. does not have very many airline companies undertaking large-scale air transport.

In Europe, air transport is based on national companies: British Airways, Alitalia, Air France, Swiss Air,

Finnair, KLM (Holland), Sabena (Belgium), Iberia (Spain), etc.

The Scandinavian countries have a unique model in this area—SAS, the Scandinavian Airlines System. This multinational company is at one time the national company of Norway, Sweden, and Denmark.

A similar construction is not known in any other country, and it has now proven itself successful for more that 40 years.

The company is owned 3/7 by Sweden, 2/7 by Norway and 2/7 by Denmark. In each country the state owns half of the national shares, while the other half is in private hands.

In size SAS is the fifth in Europe, thus holding its own in competition with the biggest companies. The three participating countries together comprise about 18 million people spread over a very large geographic area.

Thanks to the SAS model, the very word "Scandinavian" has become synonymous with high quality and service. The hard competition in air transport makes it absolutely necessary to pamper the passengers. SAS has done this so well that in 1983, it was elected "Airline of the Year," and in 1986, "Best in Passenger Service."

This three-nation company managed to have operational surplus by the beginning of the eighties while most other companies had rather large deficits every year. The main reason for this progress was that SAS launched "The Businessman's Airline"—not just as a slogan, but as an entire concept, from ticket ordering to arrival, with particular regard to comfort and service.

Another reason for the success is that punctuality, not seen before in air transport, was maintained. SAS insists that air transport must be just as punctual in departure and arrival as are the railroads.

Passengers on SAS probably experience service somewhat different from that of certain other companies. Some of the American companies have a very strong, personal, almost obtrusive style when addressing passengers, whether through information from the loud speaker or in the cabin personnel's direct contact with the individual passenger. In contrast, SAS personnel have been trained to be helpful to the utmost all right, but in a somewhat more discreet manner.

The philosophy is that a goodly number of the passengers probably wish nothing but peace and quiet during the trip. They want to rest, perhaps to read or prepare for meetings after arrival. Therefore, reserve and finesse is required of the personnel who have contact with the passengers, so that no one feels put upon with interruptions.

You might say that the golden mean mentioned at the beginning of this book in regard to communication has been accomplished in practice by SAS.

Scandinavian Airlines System operates 16 hotels in the three Scandinavian countries—three in Copenhagen, two in Stockholm, and two in Oslo. The hotel chain has been expanded with a hotel in Vienna and one in Kuwait, and several European capitals will follow before long.

One of the advantages of these hotels is that one may check into the hotel completely, avoiding standing in line upon arrival at the airport. SAS has similar services at a number of large hotels around the world—e.g., at the Plaza in New York.

The Scandinavian Airlines System has made the Copenhagen Airport the "Gateway to Europe." This airport is the largest workplace in Denmark.

In regard to selection of goods, to services and—not least—to price levels. Copenhagen Airport compares with the best and the least expensive. In 1984, the prices for alcohol, tobacco, perfume and chocolate reached bottom, yet another reason why the number of transit passengers in Copenhagen is constantly rising.

Of course, all these activities and improvements are, first of all, for the sake of air travel. The many frequent daily flights to the most important destinations in the world, coupled with punctuality and safety, have made the SAS concept a dynamic and much-admired reality.

Traffic and Communication

As former minister of transport, communication and public works, it is natural for me to give an outline of traffic policy.

The first commandment is, of course, safety. Roads, materials, traffic rules, etc., must be, first of all, adequate to secure the citizen against accident, damage to life and limb, and, secondly, against material damage.

The second commandment is practicability. Traffic—meaning transportation—can't wait. You don't start a journey for the sake of travel, but to reach your destination. The sooner you get there and back the sooner the journey is over.

People who are being transported do not want to

stay in cars, busses, taxies, trains or airplanes. They want to reach their destination as fast as possible. The same goes for merchandise and goods. The time in the railroads cars or trucks must be as short as possible. The merchandise must be fresh on arrival; if it stays in transport it costs money and makes the price higher to the consumer.

The third commandment is "room for everyone." We must have room for the "hard" as well as the "soft" road users—that is, for motorists as well as for pedestrians and bicyclists.

Therefore we have to separate them; it is not good for them to run up against each other. This is why we use large sums of money to put in bike paths in the cities and in the country. Otherwise the "hard" traffic would make victims of the "soft" road users.

(The concept of "room for everyone" does not apply only to traffic. This should be a prime rule for all kinds of legislation. Our laws must be made so that as few as possible fall through the framework of the sections of the law. We must make room also for characters, eccentrics and deviationists. As few as possible should be made criminals. But, of course, we must have traffic rules and respect them as much as other rules of society.)

The fourth (and last) commandment is choice. Our citizens, families and businesses must have available as many different kinds of traffic forms as possible. According to time, number and mass, weather, distance and purpose of the journey, there must be a number of possibilities for the immediate solution of the transport task in question.

94

Most people have a variety of traffic identities, sometimes occurring on the same day. Here you are a motorist, there you are a bicyclist or pedestrian. Here you are the driver, there you are the passenger in a bus, train or airplane. One mode is no better than the other. Room and choice among the various transport methods must be the goal of the planners.

The above four commandments taken together make up the philosophy behind a healthy traffic policy.

In Denmark the policy is quite varied. We do not have the conditions that prevail in Los Angeles. In that large city pedestrians are as rare as pearls in oysters, and it is almost impossible to get a taxi. Everyone has at least one car of his own, most families have two, so they do not suffer when one has to go to the repair shop.

During a stay in Los Angeles my wife and I went walking several times (among others on the Sabbath). While we walked hand-in-hand down the long streets, we were asked several times if we needed a lift. With interest we were asked if our car had broken down!

We found this very considerate, yes even charitable, but also very strange. We came to the conclusion that the good citizens of Los Angeles got their exercise only by jogging, or on the tennis courts or golf courses. And then we longed to be home with our bicycles!

In a small country with a coastline of 4350 miles which consists of a large peninsula and lots of small and medium-size islands, the sounds and the channels are often a troublesome hindrance to passage. For this reason the Danes have become clever bridge constructors. Dozens of bridges connect the landed areas. The longest bridge up till now—more than one and three-

quarter miles long—was inaugurated in 1985, and, because of its architectonic beauty, it has already become a
tourist attraction (the Farø bridge across the
"Storstrømmen" between Seeland and Falster).

But now we are starting a much larger project: The
connection over the Great Belt between Seeland and
Funen. It will be nearly 12½ miles in length and the
longest in Europe until one over the English Channel is
completed.

The decision to finally connect Seeland with the
rest of the country leads to the realistic planning of a
connection between Sweden and Denmark. When the
said bridges and tunnels are finished in the middle of
the nineteen nineties, Denmark will truly live up to her
natural role as a link between the Scandinavian peninsula and the European continent.

However, lots of traffic will still be sailing. . . . We
have a lot of ferries, public as well as private. There is a
certain romance connected with ferries, and they will
remain an important part of Danish traffic culture in
the future.

As former minister for communication, I had the
joyous experience of being responsible for a postal service that is indeed "second to none." Only a few other
countries can join us in guaranteeing its citizens over-
night delivery of letters from any address in the country
to any other address with a regularity of more than 95
per cent. Of the remaining 5 per cent, very few are de-
layed more than one day.

Internationally seen, this is impressive, and naturally it would be hard to improve it much. Still it is not

good enough. Is anything or anybody ever good enough?

In spite of our good results, there are complaints of delays. The Danes are accustomed to the best of service, and it is a simple fact that we are very much spoiled with our public service—and this is as it should be. You should get full value for your taxes and postage!

As everywhere else, you hear mostly—or only—about the delays. No one talks about the majority of letters that arrive in time by train or plane. They are taken for granted.

Of course the goal is 100 per cent precision. And after that what are we going to aim for? As you know, only the Russians can go above 100 per cent.

I console myself that it will always be possible to reach higher. According to a U.S. saying: When you have reached the top of the mountain—keep climbing.

Denmark, the National Park

Christian Christensen
Minister of Environment

All of Denmark is only five times larger than Yellowstone National Park. Denmark has no National Parks. There is no room for them. Eighty per cent of its area is used for agriculture and forestry. Most of the country's five million inhabitants live in cities that are small compared to American cities. Internationally seen, our industry pollutes only moderately. Compared to other, especially to large, countries, Denmark probably seems idyllic. Once when Indian Prime Minister

98

Nehru had asked how many Danes there were and was given the answer, "Five million," he sighed: "It sounds so reasonable."

On an international scale it may be said that Denmark's environmental problems also are reasonable.

Here I shall try to give a picture of the environmental problems that occupy the Danish authorities and the Danish population. At the same time I will illustrate something that is typically Danish.

Denmark is part of Scandinavia, culturally and linguistically related to Norway and Sweden. But Denmark is not like these two big brothers who are colossal in comparison, and who have vast stretches of virgin land, like the U.S.A., with mountains, rivers, large forests, tundras, islands and lakes.

Denmark has almost no virgin land. There are no mountains, and only a very small part of the country has not been touched by human hand. Everywhere there are traces of several thousand-year-old settlements and utilization of the land. Out of hundreds of thousands of burial mounds there are still about 25,000 left, and in certain parts of the country there are traces in the landscape which convincingly tell the present-day observer that he is in a very old country. In many places one can see low banks in the landscape which show how the farmers of those days grew their crops.

The country is not a natural landscape and cannot show its geological history like the Grand Canyon. But it is a blend of culture and nature, and this man-made landscape mirrors a balance typical of a landscape made and used by man for thousands of years.

The Danes themselves see part of their country as

nature. And it is true, the beaches—some of Europe's best—are untouched nature, indeed; perhaps the border between sea and land is Denmark's only "real" nature. But the Danes also think that the heaths, the large salt marshes, and in some cases also the woods, are nature.

However, these are examples of "half cultures,"of the meekly adapted way of life to which earlier generations had to adjust in areas that offered no natural riches, but only hard toil in a somewhat difficult climate.

Overgrazing and lack of fertilization created the poor heaths in the western part of the country. Almost all of these nearly deserted stretches whose sparse population had to live from modest sheep farming have disappeared. With modern technology they have been transformed into highly productive farmland, furnishing agricultural products to its own five million inhabitants as well as to the people of Europe.

However, these heaths and woods are part of what the Danes consider their "nature." They are used to this nature which has been described in literature and has formed the background for Danish life for generations. The great joy of the Danes is the landscapes and types of vegetations we have today, the traditional farmland, and the varied and numerous woods with their flora and fauna. Hundreds of thousands are members of organizations whose purpose it is to protect this man-made nature.

Thus our view of nature has a "historic" dimension. Nature in Sweden or Norway, or in the special part of the Danish kingdom, Greenland, has an eternal quality, a quality of time standing still, of nature being unchangeable. It can seem mighty, sometimes even oppressive—especially to a Dane. Danish landscape is different. In its modest dimensions it is innocent. There is never a long stretch from one place to another. Impressions change. The solitude of the woods or the great stretches of heaths are replaced by the omnipresent sea, by inlets, islands, beaches, and small settlements.

A characteristic of the farms is that they are spread around the country, in contrast to other places in Europe where the farms are gathered together in villages. These scattered farms give the country a cozy, intimate look.

Not only the landscape, but also the politics of the country is characterized by subdued compromise. The modest area, the transformation from a farming society to industrialization, and the agriculture which has changed into a kind of agricultural industry has required a balancing act. Denmark has no areas to squander away. After the Second World War, there was an explosive growth in the number of personal cars and a growth in income which brought heavy demands for city growth, for the building of new one-family houses, and for summer houses for hundreds and thousands of Danish families. For some years this development was haphazard, especially in the way the summer houses put their stamp on the countryside.

Planning and legislation led to protection of farm lands and woods from non-agricultural building, and we succeeded not only in keeping land at sensible prices for farming and forestry, but also in keeping the landscapes intact as "nature."

Parallel to this, legislation has also been put

through to protect our *natural resources*. By revising earlier laws, additional protection against pollution of ground water and raw materials as well as protection of rivers and lakes has been carried through. More stringent demands in regard to industrial emissions have stopped the rise of earlier years' increasing air pollution.

This development has been inspired by the central authorities, but it has not been characterized as central planning. It has been a political wish that this so-called planning reform and environmental protection be done with co-operation between central and local authorities, and today it is essentially the local authorities who have the responsibility for watching over our country's environment.

Of course there has been some resistance to this development, but there is growing awareness that protection of the Danish landscape is a must, not only to maintain Danish nature for everyone's pleasure, but also so Danish agriculture can maintain its high quality of production.

I began this little exposition with the paradox that there is no "real" nature in Denmark. But the nature we have is so much beloved by the Danes that they form private clubs with the purpose of working for the preservation and other protection of the blend of nature and culture that is Denmark.

And then, the last paradox. Why is the title of this chapter "Denmark, the National Park"? Because the people's interest in protecting the environment is so great that the Danish landscape is protected legislatively and administratively to the same extent as the great national parks of other nations. This is sufficient. In addition to the west coast of Jutland, a few large woods, and special preserves, the splendor of nature is spread widely. There is a strong wish that nature be protected in general, and not only in a few selected places where one can enjoy it after passing wide stretches of spoiled and neglected landscape. This probably is a natural development for a small country: One tends to make more of a small garden than a large one. This tendency can be seen in overcrowded but well-ordered Holland.

Along with the interest in protection of nature, has been the desire to safeguard our culturally historical buildings. The aforementioned sudden development of motoring and industry, and the building after the Second World War, meant that a number of cities suffered demolition of older buildings to make room for parking places. Different functions have required additions, demolitions and changes in traditional building, in the cities as well as in the country. In later years, educational campaigns, registration of historical buildings, and public grants for restoration of valuable structures have helped save more and more buildings from being demolished or neglected.

For centuries Danish agriculture was characterized by the manor house. Our country has about 600 manor houses, of which three hundred are protected. These buildings which, especially in the eastern part of the country, are so evenly spread about and are such a natural part of the Danish landscape and of the Danes' view of the landscape, that the loss of only a few of them would be unacceptable.

Together with the country's approximate 1200 village churches, of which the greatest part was built in the eleventh and twelfth centuries, the manor houses, especially those from the seventeen hundreds, are our most important architectural heritage. They are part of a European cultural tradition, but they have a special Danish characteristic, adapted to the Danish landscape of which they are part.

It is this blend of man-made landscape, the many small woods, 100,000 farms spread about the country, the traces of the activities of earlier generations, the churches and the manor houses, a better and better present and future plan for the use of the land, which is the reason why the entire country may be called—with some ironic exaggeration—Denmark, the National Park.

A conscious need for a constant balancing act between preservation and development is the basis for the maintenance of a modern society in a small area where much consideration must be taken, for there are many to share a vulnerable landscape and a vulnerable ecological system.

This balancing act may appear troublesome and enervating, but it is necessary. This is the only way we can justify the saying: "Small is beautiful."

The Freest Schools in the World

Bertel Haarder
Minister of Education

A visiting American studying Danish research and education will quickly discover a striking contrast between Denmark and the U.S.A. In general, Denmark uses many more resources per inhabitant in the Folk Schools and on youth training than it does on research and higher education. The Danes have always culti-

105

vated a broad base rather than an elite. This does not mean, however, that our elite is inferior. Many Danish researchers are of world renown. But the private sector is dominated by small establishments of which only few are strong enough to support research work. It follows then that, although the Danes desire to defend themselves with modern weapons, they do not allow weapons manufacturing on their land (as opposed to Sweden). This means that Denmark has no weapons research. Thus our total research cost is only 1 per cent of the gross national product, which contrasts sharply with the cost of maintaining the high Danish standard of living.

On the other hand, our Folk Schools are far and away the most expensive, splendid and best staffed in the entire world. In ten years the number of students per teacher has fallen from 15 to 11. (This should be viewed in light of the fact that gradually we have more employees than clients in Danish foster homes, Danish prisons, hospitals, etc.) In general, Denmark has the world record in public service—and therefore nearly a record tax burden as well.

But our Folk School is not only well-equipped and well-staffed. It is also characterized by something especially Danish—a great deal of parental rule.

Modern Denmark's founding father, N.F.S. Grundtvig (1783-1872), furnished the spiritual foundation for Danish liberalism which today is so strong that it also greatly influences the Danish political left. Grundtvig found it important to separate the state and the individual. Accordingly, his followers built independent schools and churches all over the country. First without support from the state, later with about 85 per cent state support for all expenses, including salaries— and this without any significant state control.

Ten per cent of Danish children attend such private schools with 85 per cent support. This number is so low because the public schools are also supervised by the parents.

This is the most remarkable fact about the Danish public school: It is not the minister or the municipality, but the so-called school board, consisting of parents, which decides which school books and teaching materials should be used. The school board may also have great influence on the running of the school since the municipality may leave it a grant with certain limits within which the school board has the liberty to make dispositions. The school board cannot hire principals or teachers, but it may make recommendations, and it can have a great influence on the division of the total pool of teaching hours in the school.

As a minister with a wide majority in parliament, I have carried out a number of new developments in the Danish Folk School. The school has been further decentralized, and the school board has been given still more opportunity to influence the school. In addition, it has become easier for the municipality to offer the parents a choice among its schools. At the same time I have asked the schools to create an independent profile, and to tell the parents what they stress in particular, so that through the school boards they can be held to their goals.

In Holland 50 per cent of the schools are private,

but the private schools in Holland have a lot less freedom than the public schools in Denmark!

The Danish school is the most costly, but also the
freest in the world.

Many visitors will probably think that Danish
schools stake too much on the broad base and too little
on the elite. But this is not true. Rather, Danish unified
schools and the steadily growing emphasis on individu-
alized instruction favor especially the gifted students
who have the chance to go ahead, whereas (in my opinion) the weaker students are left on their own more
than before. The result is a swelling of special training
classes which gradually are using 20 per cent of the total
resources. Among my efforts is one to give the children
more normal hours so that we can reduce the number
of children who need special training and are therefore,
much too early, made social clients in their own as well
as in others' eyes.

OECD (The Organization of Developed Industrial
Countries) has given the Danish school system top
grades, and has paid special notice to our system of having "class teachers." Through this system the children
have a certain teacher to stick to. Often it is the Danish
teacher, but in principal it can be any one of the faculty.
For some decades it was the practice to have the teacher
specialize, to teach only a few subjects. Now we are going the opposite route: The present tendency is for the
teacher to teach more and more subjects, to give the
children confidence and cohesion in instruction.

However, it would be wrong to depict the Danish
schools as an idyllic setting flowing with the milk and

honey of knowledge. Danish children are no better than children of other countries. Assaults take place in the school yard. You will find very good schools and very bad schools, and just as the children are not always good, so are the teachers not always good.

The eternal problem of the Danes is that by cultivating breadth, they risk cultivating mediocrity—and, what is worse, provincialism and self-righteousness. The Danes have an indomitable belief that deep down they are the best in the world. Therefore they turn their back on Europe while receiving large subsidies from the European Common Market (EEC), and feel it is natural that they should be defended by other NATO countries while they pay cheaply for the admission ticket into the organization.

But the Danes have begun to realize that they are part of the larger world, for better or worse. They have discovered that racism also can happen in their country. They have discovered that terrorism may show up in Copenhagen, just as in Vienna and Rome. They have discovered that they have to become international.

This is why I have stressed that our schools strengthen the teaching of foreign languages (Americans are impressed already with our present foreign language studies). I have also found it important that Danish students take their study grants abroad if they complete part of their training outside the borders. In addition Denmark has actively participated in the shaping of the European COMETT and ERASMUS programs, which foster a vigorous exchange of students and teachers among countries.

In November 1985, when I spoke to the American Educational Council in Orlando, Florida, I urged the U.S.A. to promote the exchange of students from Europe. This happened to be the day after president Reagan, during his meeting with Gorbachev in Geneva, had proposed a similar exchange with the Soviet Union.

Denmark is becoming part of the world. This does not make Denmark less Danish—on the contrary. Some of the best in Danish culture has come about when influences from abroad have been transformed by the originality and rich imagination of the Danes.

Culture?
Yes, Please

H. P. Clausen
Minister of Culture

It is difficult to give a definition of culture on which everyone can agree. This is because culture mirrors our entire way of being and way of organizing our lives, both as individuals and as a society. Its culture makes a society see itself as a community.

Through the centuries this fact has been accepted directly or indirectly in Denmark. Before the Reformation, in the sixteen hundreds, the church was the patron of the arts, attracting artists and writers whose work was needed to show its position and thoughts.

After the Reformation, art and royal power went hand in hand. In 1549 we have one of the first examples of an artist getting a travel scholarship to go abroad. At that time the king gave a young painter a stipend for a four-year stay in Germany and Italy.

The Danish kings of the Renaissance were just as enthusiastic about art as were their collegues in Europe; of course, this gave incentive to our entire cultural life. We can see it this very day, in the art and architecture of many of our cities, especially in the capital.

After 1660 the absolute monarchs continued this effort to support art and literature. One striking example is the creation of the Art Academy in 1754. The king, with the learned men of the time, had already established the Royal Danish Science Society in 1742 for the promotion of the historical, physical, mathematical and philosophical sciences.

Democracy came to Denmark in 1849. At the same time the monarchs' direct influence on art and science ceased. Interestingly enough, it was during the later part of the absolute monarchy that public support for art had reached its peak.

After 1849 the responsibility for the people's cultural awareness rested with the elected parliament. It accepted the responsibility, although state support to the arts suffered a drastic reduction. Politics made it difficult to agree on distribution of the support.

However, public economic support to culture never quite disappeared. "Pensions," called grants, were given to deserving cultural personalities, and gradually these amounts were raised considerably. But few purchases were made of the young artists' work. Not until the

112

1920's did the state again begin to provide means for the purchase of artworks, especially from young artists.

These tendencies continued till after the Second World War. In 1956 the Fund for the Endowment of the Arts was established. It supported, first, the visual arts, but from 1964, all arts were included under the fund.

One of the reasons for this was that in 1961 cultural matters were placed under its own ministry, the Ministry of Cultural Affairs. During the 25 years since then, a number of support arrangements have been established in cultural areas. We have legislation securing public support in the area of music, theatre, museums, etc.

Even athletics now comes under the Ministry of Culture. Many foreigners find this surprising, but in Denmark it seems quite natural. Athletics grew as a movement in line with all the other folk movements that characterized the Danes in the 1880s: The co-operative movement, the High School movements, the political parties, etc. Gymnastics, the earlier form for organized athletics, was closely connected with the Folk High School.

Athletics is spread throughout the country in a network of local clubs which come together under national leagues. Many of the clubs are presently or shortly having their 100th anniversaries. These organizations themselves are responsible for sports in Denmark. It is not a task of the state. The state and the cities try to set reasonable economic and physical frames for the sports. But athletics is a voluntary matter and governed by the athletes themselves.

Thus there is a very old tradition in Denmark for

some public cultural support or other. This tradition can be traced back to the fact that a number of our great cultural institutions have the designation Royal in their name. Our national library is the Royal Library. We have the Royal Theatre. It goes back to the absolute monarchy. The names of other institutions also tell of their part in public responsibility: The National Museum, The State's Art Museum, The State Library in Aarhus.

Maybe we should give the Royal Theatre a special mention here. Through tradition we have three art forms under one roof and one administration. The Royal Theatre gives plays, operas and ballets. The wisdom in maintaining this system is often disputed, but that's what we have.

The maintenance of these large national institutions is a job for the state. In addition the state supports the various above-mentioned areas. The support often occurs in economic cooperation with the counties and municipalities. In this way we endeavor to decentralize cultural offerings.

Thus theatres and orchestras in the country are supported on one hand by the state, and on the other by the counties and municipalities. Counties and municipalities in Denmark, in contrast to those in many other countries, have their own basis of taxation and tax income. During the last 10 to 15 years, this decentralization has had great economic importance. Today one-third of public support to culture comes from local contribution of the cities and counties, and two-thirds comes from the state.

Cultural support is decentralized in other ways. The state offers money in various cultural areas and thus prioritizes among them on an over-all level. Within the various areas, however, the use of the money is decided by those involved. The artists, museum staff, etc., have full independent jurisdiction in councils and boards to distribute the means and determine the cultural politics in practice.

Thus Danish culture develops politically. Of course, this says nothing at all about the culture itself, or how the Danes see it.

If I am to be venturesome, my starting point—at any rate as far as Copenhagen goes—might be a widely known tourist poster showing a smiling policeman holding back traffic with outstretched arms while a mother duck followed by her ducklings cross the street. Among the people waiting in buses, streetcars, on bikes or in cars, you see no sour faces, but only complete understanding of the mother duck's situation. If we are late to work, the boss will show indulgence, for, like other Danes, he too loves ducks—alive as well as roasted.

However, if the traffic snarl is caused by some public affair, it is something else with the smiles and understanding. Then people bare their teeth and thunder against politicians, bureaucrats, and other authorities. The Danes have a healthy and natural aversion to authorities and authority. The weapon they use against these is humor and an irony which may seem somewhat impertinent to outsiders.

To us Danes, this teasing in big or small matters is part of daily life. It is not without risk to be a politician,

115

an official, or a uniformed person in Denmark. These groups are traditionally the favorite targets of cartoonists, satirists and parts of the media.

In certain papers a good Copenhagen story easily relegates an important international event from the front page to a more modest column.

It is rather typical that the most beloved uniforms in Denmark are the Tivoli Guards, the Girl Guards, and the Royal Life Guards whose daily march through Copenhagen gives color to the everyday without directly making one think of war and strife.

Whether Hans Christian Andersen described his countrymen in his fairy tales, or whether we Danes were influenced by him, I do not know. But it's sure that "Numskull Jack" in the fairy tale with all his resourcefulness and zest for life is a popular type. So is the child who in the fairy tale about the emperor and his new clothes sees through the stilted and artificial, and the love for the little matchgirl mirrors basic attitudes that are found in our social system.

True, Denmark is small. Roughly speaking the population numbers about half that of New York. But don't think great differences of dialect and thought do not exist between the population of the various parts of the country.

To the Jutlanders the Copenhageners seem superficial, talkative, and ready with a smart comeback. Surely there is something intrepid about the Copenhagener who has a fine feeling for that which is different and original. The humorist Storm P. gave us examples of this in his drawings and inventive language when, for instance, one of his clever tramps asks:"How do you see the world situation?", and the other answers: "I can't see it, I have something in my eye."

On the other hand, to Copenhageners the Jutland-ers seem staid, heavy, taciturn, and sometimes stub-born. It is true that they are folks of few words, these westerners, but they also have humor and toughness. There's the story of a farmer from a very small town, Pandrup, which like so many other towns in Jutland is proud of its tough citizens. This farmer goes to the den-tist in the nearest city; the dentist tells him that he has to anesthetize him before treatment can start. The farmer stubbornly rejects this, noting that he is from Pandrup. The dentist starts treatment; it hurts, it hurts a lot, and finally the farmer grabs the dentist's hand and stam-mers: "Give me an injection, the truth is I am not from Pandrup proper." The farmer would not compromise his fellow townsmen.

The Danes love fellowship. It has been said that the cradle of Danish culture is the coffee table.

All kinds of clubs abound. Every self-respecting Dane is a member of one or more. Club life is tradi-tional, and it is certain that it has strengthened the Danes' fundamental faith in democracy. Democracy in Denmark is not a way of government but a way of life, and the Danes cannot comprehend that others accept anything else.

When foreigners write about our country they of-ten mention the idyllic nature of our lives. This is cor-rect. The Danes love comfort and coziness. But they have not lost the sense of quality and uniqueness.

The Danes are proud of their country's cultural heritage and personalities such as Søren Kierkegaard,

117

Grundtvig, Nlels Bohr, and Karen Blixen. We are happy when Danish art and culture manifest themselves abroad. The entire nation follows our soccer team, and we are no less enthusiastic when the foreign press praises *the spectators* at our soccer matches.

In art, culture, and recreation the teamwork between professionals and amateurs thrives to the benefit, joy, and mutual inspiration of all parties.

A Danish poet once described Denmark, "You Lilliput country, so cozy by yourself." Certainly this has been so in periods where we have not only been ourselves, but unfortunately also felt that we had enough in being ourselves. Today a greater openness to influences from abroad seems to exist, an acknowledgment that they can stimulate domestic art and culture, and a confidence also that in these areas we can hold our own in relation to other countries.

We Danes are critical in that we do not wish to have artistic and cultural messages and dogmas foisted upon us. Just as does faith in authority, so do prohibitions and guardianships have rough times in this country. This is why we try to form the main principles of cultural politics so that the greatest possible variety of options is obtained by having the state, the city, and the private sector share responsibility for it.

The Finest Social Services of All Time

Mimi Stilling Jacobsen
Minister of Social Affairs

"And then our wealth shall be great indeed,
when few have too much, and fewer have need."*

These lines were written by the Danish poet and
politician N.F.S. Grundtvig more than one hundred

*This has also been translated: "And yet in wealth far we have
gone, when few have too much, and poor are none" (by Rold
Andersen).

119

years ago. They could be the foundation for Danish social politics and Danish mentality in general. It is true that the Danes are more "middle" than many other peoples. We take the middle course—some might say that of mediocrity, which I do not agree with, however. We Danes also value—and can't do without—skill and genius.

Thus we love to say that we have one of the finest social systems in the world. And we are not the only ones who have this positive opinion. A couple of years ago, when I visited the U.S.A., I realized that we have a fine image there. We are considered to be a prosperous country with great social security, a fantastically well-organized model society. However, there were also critical voices which I could not entirely dismiss. I heard people say that, on the whole, that which is not forbidden in Scandinavia is obligatory. It is not all that bad. But it may be that there is something to this, that through many years we have built up a number of rules, regulations and systems—with the best of intentions—to protect each other. This is also the case in the social area. Security is certainly not to be sneezed at, but we can be strangled by over-protection. We Danes probably ought to think about this when we—justly—congratulate ourselves on our social system.

And how is this system compared with those of other countries?

In many ways it is like the systems of the other Nordic countries, but it is definitely different from the systems in the rest of Europe and the U.S.A. It is not only the size of the social benefits that makes the Danish welfare state something special. Indeed, our retirement

120

level is actually nothing to boast about on an international scale. However, the social benefits are generally good, and the standards in institutions and hospitals are high.

However, what is special about our system is partly that we rely heavily on the public, partly that the benefits are available to the entire population, and, finally, that benefits are paid mostly out of the general tax system. Most other countries depend much more on private intiative and on the principle of insurance.

As a consequence of the Danish system, many social benefits are considered to be free, or at least cheap compared to their costs. This, for example, is the case with day-care institutions for children, hospital stays, doctor services, help in the home and help to the handicapped.

The Danish system is good because—at least as a starting point—it benefits the weak, the sick, the handicapped and people without income. The weakness lies in the fact that it is financed by taxes. It would probably not be a problem if taxes and fees were small compared to people's income. But during the last 20 years, public spending has risen from 26 to 60 per cent of the gross national product. This is because of the great rise in the cost of social and health benefits that has been brought about because of the changes in the family structure. During this period a great many more women entered the work force, and the number of homeworkers fell similarly. This meant that a number of the functions women had performed at home were taken over by the public through the development of day-care institutions for children, care of elders, health and education. These benefits must be provided, of course, and, as mentioned, this is done mainly via taxes. The consequence of this development is a high tax burden. And many in today's Denmark have trouble accepting this burden. It is difficult for many to understand that it *costs* to live in a welfare society such as the Danish one.

One of the most typical Danes that ever was, the actor Osvald Helmuth, once told me the following story:

"A man asked his friend: What are you giving your wife for Christmas?

"Twenty-five dollars, said the friend.

"What is your wife giving you? asked the man.

"Twenty-five dollars, answered the friend.

"Then you might as well not give each other anything, answered the man.

"We don't! said the friend."

Maybe this little story says something about the reason some Danes have trouble accepting high taxes. In our well-meaning need for fairness and security, we have probably built up our social system to such an extent that in reality we go around paying social benefits to each other via our taxes. Such a system may tempt weak characters to try to take as much as possible from the public system, and to try to "tax-speculate" and work "under the table," which is quite widespread in today's Denmark.

However, this mentality of squeezing the lemon to the utmost starts a vicious circle. It causes the politicians to respond with rules, regulations, and control. Thus we have arrived at "the regulated Denmark" that we know today, a situation which is justly questioned abroad.

The more rules, the more confusion. It leads to suspicion, insecurity and new demands. Loopholes can be

found in the legislation which clever people will immediately exploit, until the holes are closed with new rules
that conflict with other rules, which then must be
changed, etc. Yes, this is how bureaucracy can grow to
such a degree that nearly everyone is dissatisfied, although the original purpose was to make everyone
satisfied. This is the defect in the Danish social system,
and yet we still feel it is one of the best in the world!

How, then, can we solve these problems which
many foreigners probably feel are bearable problems?
It is difficult to give patented solutions, but let me point
to some possibilities. We could probably learn a good
deal from the extensive voluntary social work known in
the U.S.A.

Politicians could begin by dropping some of the
regulations, prohibitions and control they have im-
posed. As far as possible we should leave the decisions
to the locals, to the grassroots officials who know where
the problems are and how they should be solved. It
would then be easier to appeal to the general generosity
and good will.

I can sum up my attitude with the following words,
which, in spite of everything, I feel fit Danish mentality,
and the words in my introduction quoted from
Grundtvig, the founder of modern Denmark:

We must rely on self-help, but not on self-
sufficiency.

We must secure the weak without strangling the
strong.

We must find the balance between the law of the
jungle and the jungle law.

Greenland—A Part of Denmark

Tom Høyem
Minister of Greenland

More than fifty years ago the Hague Court finally
and definitely decided a long-standing dispute between
Norway and Denmark (1930): Greenland was declared
Danish. In those days few thought of asking the Green-
landers, but fortunately they mainly supported
Denmark. On April 19, 1936—six years later—Senator
Ernest Lundeen of Minnesota proposed a resolution in
the U.S. Senate asking President Roosevelt to buy
Greenland. That discussion was an old one. The U.S.A.

had bought Alaska in 1867, and at that time Secretary of State Seward had proposed that the U.S.A. buy Iceland and Greenland as well.

In those days, dealing in territories was not unusual. In the years 1916-1917, Denmark sold her West Indian Islands. Part of the price was that the U.S.A. accept Denmark's right to Greenland. This happened on August 4, 1916, even though the famous Greenland explorer Peary protested publicly, pointing to the possibilities for a navy base in South Greenland, and even though England demanded first right to buy Greenland in case of a sale (on behalf of Canada). The U.S. Secretary of State used the trade of the West Indian Islands to require the breakup of the monopoly of the Royal Greenland Trade Department. However, President Wilson did not support this demand, as he did not wish to delay the trade of the islands by discussing an uninteresting area such as Greenland.

Strategic interest in Greenland rose, even though, as late as 1939, U.S. Secretary of defense, Harry H. Woodring, wrote about it: "It is a rugged, barren island, 1600 miles long and 800 miles wide, mainly covered by a more than thousand-foot-thick icecap at a height of from 7,000 to 10,000 feet, swept by arctic storms and surrounded by fog-dominated waters, tormented by icebergs and pack ice in a belt of hundred or more miles. . . ."

Then Denmark was occupied by Germany during World War II, and there was a renewed interest in the status of Greenland. Its cryolite mining was important to the aluminium industry that was vital to the production of airplanes. The flying range of airplanes was growing larger and larger, but for the many thousands of aircraft that were to be transferred from the U.S.A. to England, an intermediate landing ground was necessary. Greenland was ideal.

But Greenland was a Danish colony. If the U.S.A. claimed this Danish colony because Denmark was occupied by Germany, then Japan could claim Dutch East India on the same grounds. At the same time an American annexation of Greenland would mean that the U.S.A. was a participant in a World War which for so long it had tried to avoid.

On April 13-18, Greenland was front page material on 57 per cent of all the papers in the U.S.A. It became the symbol of the battle in the U.S.A. as to engagement or isolationism. On April 12, 1940, President Roosevelt was able to say: "I find it excellent that the American people is learning something about a subject about which very few have thought until now. The last couple of days, a lot of people have come to me asking: 'Damn it, have you looked at a map?' Of course I have looked at a map. Everybody and his neighbor has pulled out a map, and they have read the *Encyclopedia Britannica*, just as I have done."

In 1941, the Danish ambassador to the U.S.A., Henrik Kauffman, entered into an agreement with the government of the U.S.A., who thereupon undertook to supply and protect Greenland. At the same time the U.S.A. confirmed Denmark's sovereignty of Greenland, and, in return, was allowed to establish bases on the frozen island.

When the Danish Constitution was changed in 1953, Greenland's position as a colony was abolished.

Greenland became part of the Danish kingdom—just as had been the case with the Faroe Islands. Greenland and the Faroe Islands each elect two members to the Danish parliament.

The area of Greenland has not become less interesting. Its strategic and military importance is understood by anyone who looks, not only at a map, but accepts that the Earth is round and therefore looks at a globe as well. Notice the general interest in the arctic area. The Soviets have a massive fleet off the Kola peninsula and large icebreaking ships, and a submarine that can go under the ice for a long time. Notice the great research interest and the large finds of raw materials in the arctic areas of Greenland. Whether they are being used or not, their very existence is of much greater importance than was the cryolite during the Second World War.

The Greenland that the Danish government undertook to raise up to the level of a modern society was a sparsely populated country—only 21,000 people divided into 145 settlements over a 840,000-square mile area—sixty times as large as Denmark, and the size of the entire Common Market area!

The standard of living and housing was very low, and the health conditions of the population very poor. Immediately after the Second World War, the average life span of a Greenlander was only 32 years. Today it has risen to 57 years. Development in Greenland has been fantastically fast. A modern, well-functioning health service has been built up. Tuberculosis has disappeared, and a social service, a decent standard of living, and a good system of education has been established. A policy of the Greenland government has been to concentrate people, moving them over large distances from the villages to the towns in order to create the basis for a modern fishing industry.

But on the other side of the coin, we find that as a result of this policy many Greenlanders have become rootless. Unfortunately, many have also become victims of serious alcohol problems.

In Denmark, 6 per cent of the people die unnatural deaths—that is, through accidents, murder or suicide. In Greenland the figure is 32.8 per cent; true, some of the deaths are due to accidents on the sea, or as the result of natural catastrophes, but still, the figure speaks its own frightening message.

On May 1, 1979, Home Rule was introduced in Greenland, and has proved to be viable. Already, it has taken over many areas—educational, cultural, religious—and social systems, the entire Royal Greenland Trade's production, export, and supply business, as well as the technical organization and the housing department of Greenland. This means that, now, Greenland politicians have the responsibility for the administration of the island—a happy and natural development.

When Home Rule was introduced, a special arrangement was made between Home Rule and the State. It concerned non-organic resources—that is, mineral raw products, including oil, gas, and water power. According to the special administration of raw materials for Greenland, the jurisdiction of this area is joint, so that important decisions, such as granting of concessions, etc., require agreement between the Danish government and Home Rule.

This arrangement has worked well, and up till now the most important result of this co-operation has been the renewal of the search for oil in Greenland after a concession was granted to the American firm Arco (Atlantic Richfield Company) to search for and extract oil in Jameson Land in East Greenland. These efforts, which are now encouraged in agreement between the government and Home Rule, have far-reaching implications for Greenland as well as for Denmark.

Denmark will still, I believe for many years to come, have obligations and interests in Greenland. A paradox in the development of Greenland is the fact that after the Second World War there were only 370 Danes in Greenland, while in 1987 there are more than 10,000 out of a total population of 52,000 people. The more area the Home Rule takes over, the more Danes are employed there. The reason is a great lack of skilled workers. For example, about 540 teachers have been sent to Greenland. At the seminarium in Godthaab, about 25 to 30 per year are presently being trained. Thus it will take a long time before a sufficient number of Greenlanders have been trained to handle all the demanding functions of a modern society.

The entire area of health will probably remain an affair of state for a long time to come, and certain matters cannot be transferred according to the agreement between Greenland and Denmark. These are, among others, the areas of defense, foreign politics, and criminal justice—and the prison systems.

However, it is evident that we are at the beginning of a new phase of Greenland's history. Greenland's Home Rule has been established and appears to be working well. We have reached this point without shots being fired or any of the problems seen when Home Rule has been introduced to other places in the world. On the contrary, the result has been reached based on a solid cooperation established between Greenland and Danish politicians and their officials.

Greenland is in America. At one place there is a shorter distance between Greenland and Canada/North America than between the islands in Denmark. Most of the year one can even walk or go by dog sled across the narrow Nares strait.

To be completely honest, each year Greenland moves still a bit closer to North America. By means of a large radar at Sdr. Stromfjord we can send signals to Kiruna in North Sweden via the moon. In this way we are able to determine that Greenland is moving towards the American continent with about the speed of a growing fingernail.

The location and the linguistic and cultural connections with the inhabitants of Alaska and Canada, as well as the similar climatic conditions, are also the basis both for Greenland's development and for the growing wish for greater independence. Also, the new Greenland flag does not look at all like our Nordic flags.

Through the organization ICC (Inuit Cirkumpolar Conference), the citizens around the Arctic Sea try to (re)discover their identity both culturally and historically, but also in the business of daily arctic life.

130

The populations of Alaska, Canada, Siberia and Greenland share a common language.

With Greenland being one-fifth of the entire arctic area, Denmark also has some unique possibilities and opportunities.

Throughout the years arctic research has had the natural and involved interest of Danish scientists. In the future, arctic research from all over the world will be centrally placed. Polar institutes can be found in Norway, Sweden, France, England and the U.S.A.

In Copenhagen, I am visited each year by 30 to 35 American scientists who give an account of that year's American scientific projects in Greenland. These are million-dollar projects with fascinating perspectives, projects that Denmark/Greenland in no way could handle by themselves, but to which we have the key, nonetheless.

In Denmark we have a very long tradition of arctic research, primarily in regard to ethnologic, geographic and geologic research.

In 1984, President Reagan carried through an "Arctic Research and Policy Act." With this the U.S.A., for the first time, has got a really superior arctic research policy. Naturally, Alaska is the U.S.A.'s "doorstep," but a policy is needed for the entire arctic area. A five-member commission is going to prioritize and coordinate the entire input of the U.S.A. Clearly, the U.S.A. has thus taken steps to enlarge the research activities in the arctic area.

Danish scientists will continue to be in the frontline, however. We are the only country in the Common Market with direct arctic experience, and at the same time we are involved in the Nordic research collaboration. We used to say: Go West, young man. Our descendants will say: Go North to the future.

In parts of Greenland there is a great dependency on the sealing industry. The inhabitants' contact with and respect for nature is intense every day. Every day! Seals are the bread and potatoes for the Greenland sealer.

In the village of Sdr. Upernavik there lives a sealer family. They have nine children. The family lives in a very small house. They have 30 dogs. The main decoration in the home is a large color photo taken on the day the family caught 53 seals in one day. The wife prepared them all—the meat and the skin. The 25-year-old son, the oldest, now has his own house. He is becoming a great hunter.

The sealers in North and East Greenland all agree that the stock of seals is growing steadily. Still Europe and the U.S.A. are attacking the sealing industry. What can we do about the detrimental campaigns of the large, rich, multinational environmental organizations? Why don't they attack the slaughter of lambs, or calves, or pigs? Of course, we all know the answer. The attacks are led by people to whom sealing has no importance at all, and the sealers organizations are completely unable to answer the attacks. The campaign against sealing has totally ruined the prices of seal skins.

It is difficult to explain. A sealer has taught his 15- or 17-year-old son that sealing is his future, his identity, his inheritance and tradition. Suddenly the catch cannot be sold. Why? ask the young people. "Because Europe and the U.S.A. are against the life values I have taught you," the father must answer. Why? asks the young one. "Because they say there are not enough seals and whales." The young man can go down to the sea and see growing flocks of seals every single day—and large flocks of whales every season. What happens to the young man's feeling of identity? What happens to that society?

In 1985 the president of Greenland, Jonathan Motzfeldt, wrote: "It is not our political goal to live like the old Eskimos in closed reservations—isolated and backwards in relation to the rest of the world. . . . Many friends in the industrialized world seem to have misunderstood this. I will go as far as saying that there are many well-meaning people, including scientists, who want to force a certain romantic viewpoint on us. But in my opinion, we should not become substitutes for the dreams of others. We have our own dreams, and we have fought to realize them, and we will realize them, gradually, as we get enough influence to do so."

Epilogue

Compromise, Doubt, Belief

"There is something rotten in the State of Denmark." So reads Shakespeare's famous line from *Hamlet*, which inspired the title of this book. Today many Danes will spontaneously subscribe to this description, but they only appear to mean it. In reality, the vast majority is satisfied with the state of affairs.

I have given a talk titled "The Good Old Days—What Happened to Them?" in many parts of the country and in many different circles. In this talk I maintain that everyone in our society is better off than his parents or grandparents ever could have dreamt of being. This does not apply only to technology, education, and health, but to the entire social sector; it applies to leisure

134

time, to freedom, and to society's offerings in culture, training, and entertainment. It especially applies to economics, which, as we know, forms the basis for many new opportunities.

Not once during these many discussions on this subject have I been able to provoke anyone to admit that it was easier or better in the old days.

When the Danish Minister of Finance goes abroad to obtain loans on the international market, he is very welcome. There is practically a line of consortia willing to lend money to Denmark, and this in spite of our much-too-large foreign debt. The confidence in Denmark is very great—abroad as well as at home!

Also, international studies and comparisons always show that the average Dane is among the most satisfied of all the citizens in the world.

Prince Hamlet is also famous for another line: "To be or not to be?" Here Shakespeare hits the mark. The Danes have more doubt than belief. They hesitate rather than act too soon.

It is this very doubt and skepticism that makes up the nations's strength. It is a vaccine against extremes. In between, when doubt is conquered, the Danes show strength and originality.

The doubt leads to a desire to experiment. In his book *To Seek a Better World*, Robert F. Kennedy said: "The essence of the Kennedy heritage is a will to experiment, to dare, and to change, to hope the uncertain and to risk the unknown." This characteristic applies very well to the Danes. A five-fold confession to the value and necessity of experimentation.

Doubt and experimentation lead to compromises.

Epilogue

In the democratic (political) debate, the concept "compromise" is often disparaged. A compromise, some say, is a solution in which no one is really satisfied.

But isn't it true that without compromise one can't live with other people. In marriage, in friendship, when working together—be it in an organization, a business, or on an athletic team—honorable compromises must be made. If you are not willing to do so, you will have to move to one of the 400 uninhabited islands in Denmark or become a hermit somewhere else.

The Danes are champions in compromising. In an earlier chapter I described the Danish multi-party system. In spite of the many parties and the traditional minority governments, the Danish democracy and the Danish society is amazingly stable. This observation has been made by many foreign observers.

The many parties may be related to our desire to experiment. In a time when technology develops by leaps and bounds, changing our way of life from decade to decade, in a time when inherited values are constantly being tested, it is also natural that the political pattern be characterized by experimentation. Perhaps theories, systems, and parties that are 75 or 100 years old do not have the right answers to today's challenges. In this area many larger countries could learn something from Denmark. Lately, even in tradition-bound England, there are signs of a break-up of the old pattern.

Standardization leads to stiffness and stagnation. Doubt is healthy, experiments are life-giving, and the ability to compromise assures our belief that a good society can always be made even better.

ABOUT THE AUTHOR

Arne Melchior is a leading member of the
Danish Parliament. He created this volume
while serving as Denmark's Minister of
Transport, Communication and Public
Works. In this job he directed the affairs of the
Telephone Company, the Post Office, SAS, the
buses, the taxis, the waterfront, the roads, etc.
In all, he supervised 75,000 employees.

Mr. Melchior's father, Marcus Melchior,
was Chief Rabbi of Denmark and the author of
A Rabbi Remembers. Under the Nazi
occupation of Denmark during World War II,
the Melchior family played a major role in
Denmark's saving of more than 90 per cent of
its Jewish population.